Closing the Deal

Closing the Deal

TWO MARRIED GUYS
TAKE YOU FROM SINGLE MISS
TO WEDDED BLISS

Richard Kirshenbaum & Daniel Rosenberg

with cartoons by Marisa Acocella Marchetto

William Morrow *An Imprint of* HarperCollins*Publishers*

Before we go any further, please note that all names in the examples used in the book, except for quoted interviews, have been changed to protect the innocent. Therefore, if you recognize yourself in any of the examples, it's not because it *is* you (get over yourself)—it's because this stuff is universal. Or your best friend is a gossip.

HarperCollins books may be purchased for educational, business, or sales promotional use. For information please write: Special Markets Department, HarperCollins Publishers Inc., 10 East 53rd Street, New York, NY 10022.

FIRST EDITION

Book design by Shubhani Sarkar

Cartoons copyright © 2005 by Marisa Acocella Marchetto
Title spread photograph copyright © by Getty Images

Printed on acid-free paper

Library of Congress Cataloging-in-Publication Data

Kirshenbaum, Richard, 1961–
    Closing the deal: two married guys take you from single miss to wedded bliss / by Richard Kirshenbaum & Daniel Rosenberg.
        p.   cm.
    ISBN 0-06-059009-2 (alk. paper)
    1. Dating (Social customs)   2. Mate selection.   I. Rosenberg, Daniel, 1970–   II. Title.

HQ801.K573   2005
646.7'7—dc22   2004057901

05 06 07 08 09 DIX/RRD 10 9 8 7 6 5 4 3 2 1

To **Natasha, Talia, Georgia,** and the next generation of deal closers everywhere.

And to **all girls** who dream about their wedding day.

Contents

Introduction

YOU KNOW HER.

She's a smart, attractive woman with a great sense of humor and a shoe closet to match. She may be your best friend, your colleague, or even *you*.

It's not that men aren't interested. They are. In fact, there have been quite a few men along the way. Not over double digits, mind you. She's still a lady, albeit a modern one. Sure, men have a habit of sniffing or sticking around, but why can't *she*—or, better yet, *you*—get that everlasting commitment? Why can't you close the deal?

We're glad you asked.

What you really need is a guy's opinion. Or, perhaps, two guys' opinions: men who were single and afraid of commitment but who traveled to the Other Side, men who came to the eventual realization that marriage isn't just for women and homosexuals anymore. What were the factors that contributed to our eventual change of heart? We're going to explain it to you in the same fashion that your boyfriend would, if he could only learn how to communicate.

We are two fairly sane, happily married men (spit three times, say our wives) who wanted to write a book for women who want to close the deal but may not know how—women who want to be smarter about how they approach relationships. We figured that if we could successfully bestow this knowledge upon women earlier in their dating careers, especially ones who want to experience childbirth with their spouses, then we will have accomplished our goal. And that would be a great thing for both women and the men they date.

But what, you ask, makes *us* qualified to write a book about relationships and make rash generalizations while telling you things you may not want to hear (like the truth)?

We think the very fact that we're *not* therapists, relationship counselors, doctors, or women makes us uniquely eligible to share insights that really matter. We don't know any of the impressive professional vernacular that's been "scientifically" proven to score men. We're just regular guys who know what speaks to other regular guys. Our logic is that when one decides to learn how to skydive, one should ask a paratrooper who's done it rather than a physicist who's studied it.

We have spent our lives around mothers, sisters, aunts, and other female relatives and friends, which has made us well equipped to give you the kind of advice we give to all the women in our lives— and there are many. Mostly, though, it has been our friends and (some) relatives who have successfully taken our advice and who have encouraged us to share it with the rest of womanity. In fact, just this past weekend, one of Daniel's longest projects, a woman who shall remain nameless (but she knows who she is), finally got married after handling her latest relationship like a seasoned deal closer.

We also know a lot about men—not just because we *are* men, but because it's our job to know. Between us, we have spent a great deal of our professional lives marketing to men, creating TV commercials and developing and producing movies and television shows for the male (and female) market; attending focus groups, reviewing research, and looking at trends. No, we are not about to say that you have to use marketing techniques to sell yourself and the idea of marriage to your man. We are, however, going to suggest that there are interesting parallels between the two situations.

Think about it—the dating phase is as much about falling in love as it is about showing your mate how wonderful and compatible you are and how marvelous marriage will be.

Sure, in the process of writing this, we read reports and talked to people, but in the end, we knew that we weren't writing a diet book, so we didn't need to check with professionals. We wanted to write something practical—not give theoretical opinions in overly romanticized prose. So what you will read is what we learned from years of just being men, and being around men and women.

Perhaps you have a close girlfriend in your life in whom you trust and confide. If you do, you are lucky. But that doesn't make her your best ally in closing the deal. Every day thousands of women give other women advice about men and marriage. And so, every day, thousands of innocent relationships are jeopardized. Women who *could* be happily married are led astray by other women who know little about the male gender. We can't even count the number of times we've heard single women give their friends the worst advice about men, like to end a relationship before its time or to encourage them to give ultimatums. While these women may mean well, they just can't help giving the wrong advice because they don't know any better—because they don't know men. Misreading the most obvious and core differences on how men get satisfaction out of a relationship causes women to fail in their dealings with men. And that's where we come in.

One of the key skills that professional marketers use when selling a product or an idea is *understanding their target audience*. Because you will be selling the idea of marriage to your guy, and in this case your boyfriend is your *main target*, understanding him is the key to closing the deal. And who better to help you do this than two dudes who understand how significant this connection is? We're going to teach you how to take a look at your boyfriend and your relationship and unearth what it's going to take to make each other happy and to get him not only to start thinking about marriage but *actually* proposing it.

Of course, there are quite a few things that you probably know already. In fact, allow us to pay you a compliment: When it comes to relationships, women are smarter than men. But we're here to tell you that it *doesn't* matter that you know more about and are better at relationships than men. What *does* matter is your willingness to truly understand what men think about relationships, marriage, and commitment. This isn't about game playing or memorizing rules. This is *not* about outsmarting him to the altar. This is about understanding the gender you think you want to shack up with for the Rest of Your Life! Learning to understand him will help you close the deal—and keep it closed.

One of the most popular questions we get asked is "How long do I wait for a proposal?" It's a question that has haunted many women for ages. Men rarely, if ever, have to think about this issue—the biggest question we have in the dating phase that starts with "How long" ends with "before you let me unzip that?" (We know: It's *not* fair.) When to stay and when to leave are complicated issues that we'll cover in the book. The good news is that if you're already asking this question, then you have at least one of the deal-closing skills you're going to need.

We want you to ask the tough questions, just like guys ask themselves the tough questions. What we have found in writing this book is that men are generally more cautious than women when entering marriage. Generally, women tend to focus on the positive short-term aspects of marriage: the romantic engagement, unforgettable wedding, and memorable honeymoon. Men, on the other hand, commonly focus on the more serious long-term aspects of marriage: the monogamy, financial burdens, possibility of divorce, and, might we mention again, the monogamy. Part of being a successful deal closer will be assuaging your boyfriend's fears and refocusing him on the positive aspects of marriage. A married friend recently passed along to us an interesting observation she'd made among her very extended social circle of married friends. In almost all of the marriages where the couples were about to get or getting divorced, it was the *woman* who wanted to end it. This could be for a variety of reasons, but we suspect it's because when the man proposed, he had already spent a good deal of time thinking through and eventually accepting what a lifetime of marriage would be like, while the woman focused on the more short-term ramifications. We think this is a revealing insight, and a good example of the kind of thing you may want to take it into consideration when closing the deal.

Men should not be the only ones weighing the magnitude of this merger. You'll want to understand him and the relationship you're in so that once you do close the deal you'll keep it closed, which is what *Closing the Deal* is really about. Your goal should not be the rock on a ring. It should be everlasting satisfaction with your man.

In expanding our point of view (for your benefit as well as ours), we decided also to interview women who have had successful relationships and others who have not. Hopefully, we'll show you how to get on the path and avoid the pitfalls. Their situations may not match yours 100 percent, but perhaps you'll see some enlightening similarities. In any case, we're sure you'll be able to take away some eye-opening concepts. We've made sure that our range of women was broad—from a shrink to a famous Miss America—and they're all deal closers. Straight from the source, you're going to hear how they did it.

Alternatively, there are other couples we have witnessed over the years—a small sample of friends and acquaintances—for whom Love at First Sight occurred. Since we know these couples personally and can vouch for their relationships, we can honestly say that their union *was* meant to be. There were no big questions, no issues. They just *knew*. This book *isn't* for them. *Closing the Deal* is *not* for the meant-to-bes. Other than these few sentences, we will not write about these people again. They got lucky. They know it and we know it. Screw them.

We hope to guide and support you and help you to avoid some

of the hazards out there. Some chapters may make you angry and some may cause you to reevaluate yourself or your relationship. At times you may find this book flippant or you may find it intelligent (we're optimists), but our experience is that the truth is always easier to hear with a poke in the ribs. So if you find yourself in a place where you barely find any humor in your current situation, then you picked up our book just in time.

The most important thing is that this book gets you on the road to successful deal closing. You will learn that closing the deal isn't about being the prettiest, thinnest, most stylish, or richest woman in the room. There *is* an art to it.

So if you're a woman who would risk the cost of a book for a chance at everlasting happiness, who would take a leap of faith with two guys you hardly know, or who's willing to admit that there are a few things you don't know about men . . . then continue reading, because you may already be a better deal closer than you think.

Closing the Deal

I   *Is He __not__ The One?*

IS HE THE *ONE?* THIS IS THE SEMINAL QUESTION that always makes the act of dating both frustrating and fascinating. While this guessing game will always keep things interesting and mysterious, it may be more reasonable to tackle the *other* question first, the one that is far easier to answer: "Is he *not* The One?" While some of you would argue that you "know right away" whether someone isn't for you, sometimes it's not all that clear.

For those of you who want to get married, there actually *is* something worse than singledom: spending your life with someone who doesn't make you happy. Before we get started with your journey of self-discovery, let us emphasize that marriage isn't about entrapment. It's about taking something great and making it better. And as in fairy tales, the important part is as much about finding the *right* prince as it is about living happily ever after. Just because you think you have a prince now, doesn't mean *he's* your Prince Charming.

We're going to help you figure out where you stand with your man and help you make an informed decision by presenting the tools that will help you correctly analyze the *level* of person whom you are with. *Level* doesn't refer to social standing or self-worth, it refers to your *compatibility* as a couple and his *willingness* to commit. Besides compatibility issues, we're going to discuss *reality* issues, as well. Realities in relationships are sometimes difficult to see (especially when you don't want to face them), so we're going to spend a little time figuring out if you are being honest with yourself about your relationship.

Let's face it though, there are endless reasons why your relationship could falter before your saunter to the altar. We want to say up front that no matter how great the advice is in this book, and no matter how closely you follow it, there are some guys who will never pull the trigger. These men have **Commitia,** a type of VD (vow disavowal) that makes the most eloquent of men flub their lines at the mere mention of the M word. These are the perennial bachelors, serial daters, and commitment-phobes who exist in every socioeconomic group, and their modus operandi is fairly consistent. They certainly will never be The One. These are the relationships that need to be cut short immediately or, better yet, ended before they've begun, or else time's a-wastin'.

Let's tackle the issue of whether your man is the marrying kind—you need to know that from the start. Since the goal of *Closing the Deal* isn't to get you married for marriage's sake but to help you make that step with your soul mate, we wouldn't be doing our job if we didn't address the very difficult issue of whether you're kidding yourself about your current relationship. This is where our big brother advice really kicks in, and it won't be fun. Although we promise to be as gentle as possible, be forewarned: You could discover some great and some not-so-great news over the next few pages.

Does your boyfriend fit into the "kind of, maybe" category? Does he lack the most basic qualities that being a husband will require? Let's take the all-important "What Kind of Man Is He?" test and find out before it's too late.

The "Gloom or Groom in June?" Quiz

1. How does he view the institution of marriage?
   a. He compares marriage to a prison sentence and thinks being divorced like his parents is something to look forward to.
   b. He thinks marriage is for pushovers.
   c. When he talks about the benefits of marriage he uses phrases like "tax savings" and "combined net worth."
   d. He invites you to his grandparents' fiftieth wedding anniversary and tells you how he admires their mutual devotion.

2. What is his overall level of emotional maturity?
   a. When something goes wrong he blames you.
   b. He throws a tantrum when you don't put him at the kids' table.
   c. He uses sock puppets to talk things through.
   d. When something goes wrong, he takes it in stride.

3. How do you fight?
   a. He predictably starts with a few jabs and then goes for a weak-ass uppercut.
   b. He hits below the belt, emotionally.
   c. His mother and lawyer handle his affairs.
   d. It's strained, but civil.

4. How did he act when you got sick?
   a. He told you to sleep on the couch since he doesn't want to catch what you have.
   b. He brought you a doggie bag from the strip club buffet.
   c. He told you to go to work anyway. Someone has to support him.
   d. He stayed by your bedside and brought you chicken soup.

5. How does he treat the waitstaff in the restaurant?
   a. He barked at the sixty-five-year-old waiter, "Get me a cup of coffee, boy."
   b. How would you know? He never takes you to restaurants.
   c. He makes special requests for everything he orders, including explaining how he likes his water.
   d. He tips well and says "please" and "thank you."

If you didn't get all *d*s, then you may have to seriously consider throwing this fish back until it's grown up enough to eat. If he doesn't have the basics, he may not be worth any effort at all.

Now that you've taken the quiz, though it's simple, you're now on your way to evaluating the type of man you're with. Let's get a little deeper into dealing with your compatibility.

We Belong Together Like Ham and Eggs, Except He's Kosher and I'm a Vegan

MAYBE YOU'RE GREAT AT MATCHING YOUR shoes with your purse. Or maybe you've been the most popular gal in your clique of girlfriends. Or maybe you're great at setting up other people on blind dates. But why is it that when it comes to evaluating whether you and your future husband are a match, all of your sensible instincts seem to disappear? It could be for a variety of reasons. As easy and natural as it is to assess why someone isn't right for you, let's start by wondering if *you're* not right for someone else. In shopping lingo, let's spend some time looking in the mirror. Let's talk about you.

What is your history with men? Are you a polymonogomist or a monopolygamist? In other words, do you have a history of long-term relationships or have you been on one long stream of bad dates since puberty? Having had at least one long-term relationship to your credit is a good sign that you have a decent foundation and understanding of what a successful relationship requires. You probably understand the value of things like trust, honesty, loyalty, and every other crucial relationship ingredient. But what if you haven't had any successful long-term relationships? There could be a compatibility issue on *your* part that you are ignoring.

There are a million reasons why you might not have had a successful relationship, and quite a few of them might be completely out of your control. You may have had really bad luck when it comes to meeting men. Maybe you live on a farm hundreds of miles from the nearest town, without telephones or the Internet and are under house arrest for your unusually close relationship with your horse. Or maybe you've just made some pretty bad choices. Which leads us to . . .

Overdating and Underdating

IF YOU HAVE NOTICED A CERTAIN PATTERN in your unsuccessful past relationships, it's possible that there's something more complicated going on than simply a string of bad luck. Maybe you're **Underdating**, that is, dating someone who doesn't challenge you. Maybe he's below your intelligence (e.g., he's good-looking but conversations with him have put your venti latte to sleep); or, perhaps worse, you're **Overdating**, setting your sights too high with a guy who will never commit (e.g., you're on your knees in the Oval Office and he's also married). Just because you're Overdating or Underdating doesn't mean you can't close the deal with the guy. It just means that it's unlikely and even if you did, you might later regret it.

Overdating: Shooting for Something That Will Never Happen

Overdating is the circus mirror of relationships because there's a certain amount of distortion involved. Perhaps it's the influences of the media or our culture, but we can't tell you how many women say to us, "Can't you find me a guy who looks just like [fill in name of hot guy of the moment] or has the bank account of [fill in name of latest billionaire]?" Sure, Demi.

Be honest. How realistic are your expectations with your current boyfriend? We're not suggesting you can't land a guy that people tell you is out of your league. What we *are* telling you is that having unrealistic expectations or getting deeply involved with a man who gives you every indication that marriage isn't in the cards is not good for your ego or your sanity. You're Overdating when you're with someone who is not interested in moving forward with you and is therefore an improbable match.

Overdating isn't necessarily about you—it's about him. You're Overdating if the guy you're with has a very recent history of playing the field or has a lifestyle with a penchant for all things bachelor that shows no signs of strain. You are Overdating if his idea of getting away from it all includes getting away from *you*. Listen to what men say; most men will tell you the truth up front. For example, if he says, "For years women have tried to tame me and failed, but you're welcome to give it your best shot," you have to consider that you may be in for a long haul.

We've seen lots of women who have great skill in assessing other people's relationships but rarely look inward. These women can be the worst Overdating repeat offenders because they ignore the truth. Erica is a good example of that.

Erica

ERICA (HER NAME has been changed like all the other examples but especially because her lawyers are bigger than our lawyers) is an above-average-looking girl who knows how to enjoy life. This is partly due to her father, a multi-kachillionaire, who has bought her everything money can buy, including a few minor plastic surgeries. Needless to say, the house in the Caribbean, the oceanfront estate in Martha's Vineyard, and the yacht all make Erica even more "attractive" to quite a few men.

Erica is also known for her generosity and her quick wit. She has plenty of friends, but when it comes to boyfriends, Erica always finds herself Overdating. Erica has a Daddy complex. Neither she nor her dad realize that Erica has been trained to *not* accept a regular, nice guy. She's been told her whole life (and thus she now believes) that she deserves only the best in life, including the social status of the men she dates. This all leads to one of two situations: either Erica dates no one because she can't find anyone she feels is worthy, or, when she does date, she won't settle for someone unless he has it all—including Daddy's approval.

Although he wasn't megarich, Erica would rather have dated Drew than go out with someone who was more appropriate for her. Drew's father was a famous artist and he grew up around interesting, worldly people. He was used to women throwing themselves at him—someone once said, "He's like James Bond, except cooler. And hotter." (Can one be cold *and* hot?) He'd been surrounded by wealthy people his whole life and was used to the trappings. When he wasn't staying at the summer homes of his father's friends or dating their daughters, he was always invited to dinner parties because he had the rare combination of looks and charm.

Drew and Erica dated for about a year, spending almost all their free time together. They had a solid friendship and Daddy loved Drew's pedigree and reputation as a hot commodity. He often heaped praises on Erica for "reeling him in." Erica loved Daddy's approval. Of course, it only added fuel to Erica's Overdating fire.

Although Drew liked hanging with Erica, it was clear to everyone around them that Drew was more interested in the perks than the person. When Erica tried to spend time alone *with Drew,* he *withdrew.* He enjoyed the great dinners, the trips to her family's ski house, and the rest of the pampering, but sunset walks on the beach were out of the question.

Erica desperately wanted to get closer to Drew and to discuss their future. It was a conversation so removed from where Drew was in his life that at first he couldn't understand what she was getting at. Drew's father didn't get married until he was fifty-one, and Drew wasn't planning on beating him by more than two or three years. Whenever Erica broached the subject, Drew told her exactly where he stood, which pretty much put an abrupt end to the conversation. Drew stuck around long enough to create some fond memories, but when he heard the word on the street that Erica was expecting a rock, he hit the pavement.

While it's hard to feel bad for Erica with her lifestyle, she was truly misguided in her attempts to find a husband. Erica was used to getting everything she wanted and was sure that Drew would come around and be seduced by her personality and means. But she was dreaming about building a playpen for her future children while dating a guy who was dreaming about partying at the Playboy Mansion. Don't despair, however—all is not lost for Erica.

Overdating can be cured once you make an honest evaluation of your compatibility for the long term. Once you realize that you're not being realistic, move on. Erica had a great time with Drew and had no regrets, but after a year she realized that she and Drew were better off as friends. They still hang out occasionally, when Drew isn't loafing around his friends' Carribbean villas or staying at his new girlfriend's parents' chalet in the Swiss Alps.

Overdating is just half of the equation. Thinking you're too good for most of the single people you meet is fine if, for the most part, you are. But dating people in order to make yourself feel better about yourself won't do you any good either. We have a name for it. It's called . . .

Underdating

Underdating may have a lot to do with self-esteem. Underdaters are women who are with men who do little more than give women a boost of confidence. We've seen women who have maintained relationships with men solely to prove to the world (and to themselves) that they can score a handsome guy, a professional athlete, or a jet-setter. Underdaters date guys they normally wouldn't think twice about if the guys didn't possess one specific quality that they crave (e.g., looks).

Still not sure if you're an Underdater? Ask yourself a few questions: Does he challenge you to be a better person? Does he bore you to tears with the same stories about his high school sports victories? Is the best thing you can say about him is that he's . . . energetic or good in the sack? You're Underdating if you're dating someone who doesn't bring anything to the party.

We see many women fall into this trap. One of them is Jillian.

Jillian

JILLIAN IS A THIRTY-SIX-YEAR-OLD WOMAN who would love to still have a subscription to *Tiger Beat*. While she makes a nice living for herself as a graphic artist, this Midwestern native doesn't really care about money, hers or her boyfriends'. Jillian does, however, care very much about looks. She still gets "crushes" on good-looking actors and ballplayers and has been known to try to get backstage at concerts, if you know what we mean. While Jillian has always had a man in her life, she's the type who gets bored easily and moves on quickly. This only makes Jillian more frustrated, since marriage is what she really wants (or so she says).

Her latest *flavor flave* is Brad, an out-of-work actor/rapper who, according to Jillian, is "cut." Jillian loves the rush she gets when she and Brad walk into a room and all eyes turn. Nothing makes her happier than when other women compliment her on Brad's appearance. But Jillian is a working woman, and when the weekend comes along she often chooses not to see Brad unless there's an opportunity to show him off.

Most of Jillian's girlfriends are married or engaged, leaving Jillian more frustrated about her inability to close deals. Her habitual Underdating is the main reason. In her heart, Jillian knows that Brad isn't for her. Sure, he has a toned bod and they enjoy going out together, but the similarities end there. We happen to know why Jillian is going through her Underdating phase. She was in a four-year relationship that ended badly when her boyfriend left her for a younger woman. Jillian started to date men who got her noticed but never anyone who challenged her. She knew that if any of her recent dates dumped her she could always justify to herself that even though he was hot, he wasn't right for her in the first place.

Jillian eventually realized that she was in a terrible cycle of incompatible boyfriends and unhealthy relationships and understood that everything she was doing was only hurting her chances of closing the deal. She's not married yet, but she is dating someone from work with whom she has a lot in common.

NOW, THERE'S NOTHING WRONG with Overdating or Underdating if you're not looking for a commitment. These relationships can be fun, sexy, and exciting, but beware of getting into a pattern here. Certainly the Samantha character on *Sex and the City* was a serial Underdater, but she knew she was in it only for the sex. It was fun to watch her sexcapades, but for the average girl this behavior could take a toll on her reputation and biological clock. Maybe it got Samantha what she wanted in the end, but girls, if you're getting your dating advice and unrealistic expectations from television, repeat this mantra to yourself daily: "Just because it happens on TV doesn't mean it's gonna happen to me." If you think you're in a relationship with a guy who deep down you know is a fling who should be far flung, it's time to put an end to it.

I Hate It When He . . .

CAN YOU HEAR YOURSELF SAYING THIS? IF only he would . . . just change his style, stop being so cheap, spend more time with me, do the dishes in the sink, lower the TV volume, raise the temperature in the bedroom, get new friends, stop watching *Punk'd* (he's forty), stand up to his coworkers, listen to my expert guidance?

Do you know automatically how you'd finish the phrase "I hate it when he . . ."? How many really strong reactions come up? How many complaints instantly fill your brain? If you're already in a blind rage, it might be time to realize he may *not* be the one. We're not suggesting that you need to end it because you can't agree on what TV shows to watch or he likes the car ten degrees colder than you. But if you've reached the point in your relationship where you find it difficult to be in the same room with your boyfriend for extended periods of time without wanting to pull your hair out, then you should start to rethink some things.

If you are questioning the soundness of your relationship, he may not be the one. However, if you're the kind of person who doesn't often ask herself tough questions, we're going to save you from yourself. Let's take a little quiz to see if your relationship has the minimal requirements for the long haul.

The "I Still Think He's The One" Quiz

1. What does your boyfriend stare at during sex?
(If you're not having sex, skip to question 2 and loosen up a bit.)

    a. your eyes
    b. your breasts or butt
    c. your favorite porno
    e. his BlackBerry

2. When you plan a vacation you agree
   a. on a location
   b. on twin beds
   c. on adjoining rooms
   d. to meet up when you get back

3. What do you most enjoy doing together?
   a. staying in bed and cuddling
   b. reading
   c. squeezing his backne
   d. fighting until permanent injury or death

4. If he was incarcerated for ten years for insider trading, you would
   a. proclaim his innocence and your undying loyalty, and remain faithful to him
   b. write him a letter once a month
   c. support him at the parole-board hearing—if it doesn't interfere with your workout schedule
   d. encourage Bubba, his cellmate, to "go for it"

5. When you ask him, "Does this dress make my ass look fat?" he says:
   a. "No"
   b. "Nah"
   c. "Not really"
   d. "No, your fat ass makes your fat ass look fat"

6. You can't wait for Saturday night because it's
   a. date night with your boyfriend
   b. double date night with your friends
   c. girls' night out with your best girlfriends
   d. boyfriend-swapping night

7. You are annoyed with him when he
   a. calls you to see that you got home safely
   b. doesn't put the toilet seat down
   c. checks out other women in front of you
   d. comes near you

8. When your boyfriend calls you on his way over after work, you count the
    a. seconds until your doorbell rings
    b. hours you've been apart
    c. years you've been dating
    d. men you've slept with since he left for work
9. He embarrasses you when he
    a. tells you he loves you in front of your friends
    b. wears his docksiders with his suit
    c. picks fights with your ex-boyfriends
    d. threatens to kill one of his hostages
10. When someone asks you what your favorite thing is about your boyfriend, you respond:
    a. "Everything"
    b. "His hairline"
    c. "His crotch"
    d. "The fact that he puts up with all my bullshit"

Your score:

Give yourself 3 points for every *a* answer, 2 for every *b* answer, 1 for every *c* answer, and 0 for every *d* answer.

24–30 points. It's prenuptial time. Call the wedding planner, alert Vera Wang, and write a letter to Weddings c/o the *Today* show.

18–23 points. Very promising indeed. Start your wedding diet now.

12–17 points. A little therapy and you two are on your way.

0–11 points. At least you're getting laid.

Even if you got a whole 30 points, congrats—but keep reading.

Maybe He *Could* Be The One

WE KNOW IT'S A HARD PILL TO SWALLOW, but there are certain types of men who just don't want to be institutionalized. They're just having too much fun, and why not? Consider yourself lucky if your *he's-not-The-One* boyfriend has flat-out told you that he doesn't plan on ever getting married and nothing you can say or do is gonna change that. And, ladies, if you hear that, don't go with your first instinct (you know, to set him straight). Don't even think about fighting it. Even if the odds are fifty-fifty that you *can* set him straight, those are some pretty lousy odds when the downside could mean a lot of wasted time with a guy who can honestly say "I told you so."

Now there are also some men who do want to eventually, kind of, maybe, get married. Most men fall into this category, so let's say you're with one of those. How do you know where your man stands in all of this? How do you know if he'll eventually come around?

Is he truly incapable of discussing marriage at all? If he is, that's a telltale sign that you have a long road ahead of you. If, when you do manage to get serious with him, he speaks in vague generalities and it doesn't really matter to him how long you've been together, then that's a red flag that you can't ignore.

There will always be things that he will say, subtle or not, that will shed some light on what he's thinking. When looking at apartments bigger than one bedroom, does he refer to other bedrooms as the media room, library, and office? Does he call his engaged guy friends "disloyal motherfucking sellouts"? Hmm. When you bring up your future, does he get excited and start talking about intergalactic travel?

Look at his lifestyle, too, not just his words. Does he tend to do a lot of things on his own or without you? If he's continually living the life of a bachelor and has made little in the way of relationship concessions (like if he spends more time at work or with his friends and less time with you and/or your family), it's not a great sign.

The "One Good Excuse" Rule

GUYS ARE ENTITLED TO SPEND A GOOD DEAL of time deciding if *you're* the one. He may be vague and tell you that he's not ready, or your kind-of-maybe-wants-to-get-married-type might have a few detailed excuses as to why marriage is not in the cards right now. But the more excuses he uses, the more likely it is that they're not real. We call this the "One Good Excuse" Rule, because usually real excuses don't come in pairs. If it's that his parents don't like you and he's afraid of causing a rift in his family and being disinherited, fine (that's one excuse— long, but still logically related). If it's that *and* that he's not financially secure *and* he swore to his paternal grandmother that he would marry only a Polish ballerina *and* when she keels over he'll propose . . . then you must rethink his commitment to making a commitment to you.

Sometimes it's not easy to have a conversation about where a relationship stands. Other times, the difficult thing is finding out. We think it's crucial always to know the score, or bad things can happen. Just ask Stacey.

Stacey and Erol

STACEY IS A PROFESSIONAL SONGWRITER, attractive and athletic, and she has a ton of friends. In fact, most people would say that it's hard not to like Stacey. She is a wonderful hostess and is consistently doing things for people she cares about.

Erol is a successful real estate developer who was born in Armenia and came to the United States when he was three. He works hard and, if given the chance, will tell anyone about how his story is the American Dream. On the outside, he is as Americanized as anyone born here, but Erol's parents are from the old country and have made it clear that his marrying someone who isn't Armenian would be devastating to them. For some guys, their parents' blessing isn't really that important, but to Erol it means practically everything. While he loves being American, keeping Armenian culture and traditions alive is as important to Erol as it is to his family.

Stacey and Erol have dated for four years. From the very beginning, Erol often told Stacey that after a few more big deals he would be more financially secure, and he could see them having a future together. After two years of dating, it seemed that the "Armenian issue" wasn't really a big one. They were both in their mid-twenties and just starting out in their careers, and though marriage was spoken about, neither of them was very serious about it. Stacey went back to Juilliard while Erol was working ninety-hour weeks making real estate deals. They both wanted to focus on their careers, and neither of them wanted to make a serious commitment.

After three years, Stacey still didn't consider his parents' position the issue that would keep them apart. In fact, when Stacey asked Erol why they weren't getting engaged, Erol mostly focused on his financial situation. Love, Stacey believed, conquers all.

Erol happens to be one of those all-around good guys. He's generous, witty, extremely well read, and honest to a fault. Which is why when he told Stacey to bear with him, she really believed that things would change. Erol kept telling Stacey that once his income became more consistent, he would sit his parents down and have a big talk with them. He was sure they would come around once they got to know her.

But Stacey's friends cornered her and took her to task on her actions. They felt she had set herself up for failure. She became defensive because she truly felt that Erol would come around, that he was doing really well at work and he was going to tell his parents that he was moving ahead with Stacey with or without their consent. That, of course, never happened.

Though Erol couldn't deny that he was doing really well at work, he told Stacey that he was having trouble finding the right way to confront his parents. Stacey was frustrated and angry that Erol hadn't stood up to his parents or told them how things were going to be.

Financial security and tradition are great excuses, but years of dating later, what were the signs that Stacey missed? How could she not have had a realistic sense of the whole picture? The truth was that Erol was making more money than most of Stacey's married friends, even though he claimed he wasn't financially secure enough to support a family. Also, Erol spent a lot of time with his family and had plenty of opportunities to persuade his parents to accept Stacey into their lives, but he never had those talks. Stacey realized the truth—that Erol had two great excuses and just wasn't sure what he wanted—or maybe he just wasn't being honest with himself.

After four years of dating Erol, Stacey finally grasped the reality of the situation and decided to end it. At first she felt that for no good reason at all she was breaking up with her best friend, someone with whom she was madly in love. But then she realized that there was no better reason to leave her committed and safe relationship than wanting to start a family while she was still young. When it finally ended, Stacey couldn't help being a bit upset with herself for staying in the relationship as long as she did. It's not as if the signs weren't there.

We think Stacey *should* be a bit angry with herself and with Erol. Erol is a prime example of a guy with Commitia who didn't think twice about stealing important years from a woman he has little or no intention of marrying. It's not that Erol purposely put Stacey in this situation; it's just that when he thought about losing Stacey, he thought about *himself* (including his family and inheritance), not *her* best interests. Guys like Erol—even sweet ones—don't always act selflessly when it comes to dating. Erol was really in love with Stacey and was trying to figure out how to make it work with his family, but he took too long doing it, stringing Stacey along with promises and keeping her at bay by assuring her that things were moving forward.

Stacey really wanted to get married and start a family, and her years with Erol set her back in her goal to be pregnant by thirty. Should Stacey have left Erol earlier? We wish we had an easy answer. The best advice is to be honest with yourself and your feelings. When you start to question yourself about staying in a relationship and feel resentful, bitter, and all the other lousy emotions that come into play with drawn-out relationships, then you shouldn't ignore them. Stacey did, and in the end love didn't conquer much at all.

I Know Where I Stand, but Which Way Do I Walk?

WHILE YOUR MAIN FOCUS IN THE PAST MAY have been feeling out your man to see if he was The One, you can now discern if he's not.

We have all seen couples that defy generally accepted compatibility principles. Whether it's the bohemian and the businessman or the preppy WASP from Connecticut who married her college sweetheart, the Kalahari bushman, compatibility isn't just about aesthetics or others' opinions of your union.

Hopefully, by now you have a clearer idea about where you stand. Don't ignore what you uncover. Whether you're Overdating, Underdating, or just not sure he's The One, dating should not only be about having fun but also about getting answers to some very serious questions concerning your compatibility. And quickly. Put time into relationships that have promise, and walk away from those that don't. There's no point in wasting anyone's time, most importantly, yours.

Marketing Marriage 101

Getting into His Head Can Get You Wed

THE ROAD TO CLOSING THE DEAL WITH The One is paved with psychic abilities—the need to understand what men are thinking at any given time. That's why we're going to take you inside your man's head. Of course, giving head will also increase your chances of closing the deal, but that leaves twenty-three hours and fifty minutes a day to handle the rest of your relationship.

Just as an architect has a blueprint or a writer has an outline, you can create your very own marriage marketing plan, and in this chapter we'll show you how, from the first (and most important) step of understanding your target audience—your man—to grasping the essential *marriage motivators* that will cause your number one consumer—your man—to shift into *marriage momentum*. We'll reveal the subtleties of *marriage maneuvering*, thus helping you to ultimately hone your *marriage marketing skills*. Though these buzzwords may sound cheesy, bear with us. It's all going to make sense to you soon.

Marketing Is War:
Man Spelled Backward Is 'Nam

LIKE MANY OVERCONFIDENT MARKETERS, many women believe that there's no need to understand their audience as long as they can outsmart them. We think that's one of the biggest blunders a woman can make. As Sun Tzu wrote in *The Art of War*, "If you know both the ENEMY and YOURSELF, you will fight a hundred battles without danger of defeat." Although your boyfriend isn't exactly your enemy—he most likely is your best friend, lover, and soul mate—he will be the person sitting across from you in this ongoing series of compromises and negotiations. Face it: before you close the deal, he may have issues you have to conquer, so for now that makes him the "opposition." That's right, the man you get into bed with, the guy you want to father your children *is,* when it comes to closing the deal, the **Opponent.** And understanding exactly what he's thinking will help you take him from the "Opposition" to the "Proposition."

Your Target Audience of One

WHETHER IT'S MARKETING A NEW PRODUCT or promoting a new blockbuster, one of the first things we need to do is get a feel for the target audience. If you really want this in classic marketing terms: we attempt to understand the product's "proprietary benefits," so there is a unique, ongoing understanding of what will appeal to the "core audience," which will lead to "achieving the sale or commitment to purchase." Right about now you're missing our friendlier buzzwords.

No matter the lingo used, advertising and marketing industries spend millions each year on focus groups to get into the heads of consumers, to understand what motivates them, what they want and respond to. While we hope you already know what makes your own personal "target audience" tick, the following exercise will help you get into the mind of your man so you can officially start the process.

Imagine you're a guy. Better yet, you're not just *any* guy; you're a desirable, witty, and basically all-around good-guy guy. For the past two years you've been dating a wonderful woman with whom you've fallen in love. You love everything about her: her warmth, her smile, her intelligence, and her dexterity in bed. Only, now, since you're a *guy*, you have different priorities and interests, and one of them is *not* dissecting your relationship on an hourly basis. In fact, since you're a man, you'll think about the status of your comfortable relationship only once or twice a year (on birthdays and/or Valentine's Day). And, when you do think about it, it's most likely with the following sentence: "I wish things could stay just like this forever." It's really as simple as that.

To a woman (and we've talked to many), marriage seems to be the next logical step and the natural evolution of a great relationship. But men generally feel that while marriage may not be the enemy, Change *is*. For most guys, relationship purgatory is quite heavenly. Most men believe that the Great Unknown—*commitment*—could be Hell.

Why is that? you may ask. What's wrong with the male mind? To get heavy and philosophical on you (don't expect much more of this), consider a question the average man asks himself when *not* thinking about sex: "Is it better to be alone (independent) or hooked up (codependent)?" We can't boil it down any further. Why would he want to commit? What's he gaining? He certainly knows what he will be *losing*. For many men, the thought of being with the same woman for their entire life is enough to send them into psychoanalysis. Though we don't have psychology degrees, we know that getting married for a man is probably the emotional equivalent to having a baby for a woman, and usually men have to go through this significant life change first. For those women out there who still don't grasp this Change = Death concept, we simply ask you to recognize that your man will be losing a great deal of freedom. Acknowledge it. Accept it.

Okay, now go back to being a woman. Hopefully, you now realize that if you want to close the deal, a seismic shift needs to happen in your man that will encourage his metamorphosis into a **Man with a Plan** (aka a guy who is ready, willing, able, and prepared to get married). That shift is something we've termed **Marriage Momentum**: a force, like inertia, that once begun will be stopped only by a powerful outside force, like his mother. This force can arrive in different ways. For some guys, it's the gradual realization that marriage is the next exit on the turnpike of his life. For others, it's more sudden, like coming around a blind curve on a mountainous road with no guardrails. In other words, Marriage Momentum may sneak up on a guy at the most inopportune, unexpected, or unplanned time. Either way, once it hits, it'll be hard to stop. Let's look at a sample relationship that will highlight some of the buzzwords in this chapter.

Cheryl and Randy

CHERYL IS A BRIGHT, attractive account executive in an advertising agency. She moved to Chicago from San Francisco after the dot-com bubble burst, and soon after that she met Randy, a sports marketing executive. Randy had always been successful with women—not exactly a player, but a man who knew what he liked and wouldn't settle. After dating for about six months, Cheryl went from sleeping over on Saturday nights to having a special place in his closet for her work clothes, and about a year into their relationship, Randy was saying, "See ya, love ya," when he went off to work in the morning. Cheryl, while not in marriage mode, was still more than pleased by what seemed in her mind to be a deepening relationship. She had first met Randy when she was twenty-seven and didn't have any expectations; however, she couldn't help but be "kind of disappointed" when Randy gave her a lovely but nonpersonal cashmere scarf for her twenty-ninth birthday. After a year and a half together, Cheryl was starting to expect a little more than a Saks Fifth Avenue muffler and a casual "love ya." Perhaps that's why she felt that weird pang of anxiety. She had reached the D.I.P., **Dating Inflection Point** (a moment in time when one questions one's current dating situation), and she had no idea what Randy was thinking.

While she wasn't freaked about turning twenty-nine (it's not exactly forty-five), this birthday just seemed to set her on edge. The year and a half had gone by so quickly, and Cheryl was pretty sure that Randy was The One, but she hadn't received any indication from Randy that marriage was where he thought the relationship was headed. Two days later her anxiety seemed to be confirmed when her friend Nicole told her to "get a move on it." At first Cheryl was pissed at her tactless (married) friend, but she knew that Nicole meant well. It made Cheryl realize that she'd better find out soon if Randy wanted to move things forward or if she was going to have to start all over again.

Later that weekend, Cheryl and Randy had dinner at their favorite Greek restaurant. Cheryl felt she needed some answers. When she casually brought up their relationship by saying how much fun she was having, Randy readily agreed they were having lots of fun. "But," Cheryl continued, "fun doesn't have the same meaning it did six months ago." Randy sensed where the conversation was headed and blurted out, "What's wrong? Everything's so great, so what's the rush?" This was a difficult moment for Cheryl. Did she really want to confront Randy in the middle of a restaurant? Was she truly ready to hear his answer?

Let's stop here for a moment and point out something painfully lacking in Cheryl's relationship: She had almost no information as to where Randy stood on the subject of marriage. Although Cheryl had broached the subject a few times before, Randy had never really addressed the topic (a skill also called Tefloning). We must also point out that since Cheryl was without any indication of where she stood in the relationship, there was absolutely no Marriage Momentum in the works. Cheryl was not the confrontational type, so she desperately needed to perform some **Marriage Maneuvering** to get some answers.

And maneuver Cheryl did. But before we tell you what she did, ask yourself how you would react to Randy's question "What's the rush?"

a. "No rush. Let's just forget I brought the whole thing up. How many U.S. presidents can you name?"
b. "Randy, you'd better be thinking 'ring' soon. And I'm not talking boxing."
c. "Rush?! You selfish, insensitive prick! I see I've been wasting my time with your pathetic, pusillanimous pansy ass for over a year."
d. "No rush. I've been enjoying hanging out with you too, Randy. That's why I really don't want to have to start dating again. But if I need to start again, I will."

Okay, the best response is obviously *d*, but let's take a look at each one anyway.

a. Change the subject. This not particularly novel approach will do nothing except delay the inevitable, not to mention hinder your ability to start maneuvering. You've been changing the subject long enough. Seize the "dais"!
b. Randy knows the issues at stake. This is the most important decision he's ever going to make. Cheryl needs to be giving Randy reasons why they should be together forever, not getting confrontational or making it about status. (Every nice young lady knows that the ring is not an end but merely a symbol of impending nuptials.)
c. Anger is a terrible thing to waste—use it sparingly. In this example, Cheryl has a great opportunity to make her point clear, but her irrational response ruins a perfect opportunity to state her case.
d. Here Cheryl plays it cool but remains firm. Not only is she not making a scene, but also she's letting him know that if he wants to win the prize, he'd better buy a ticket.

In the end, Cheryl went with answer *d,* which is why things are playing out so well . . .

Although Randy was initially shocked and speechless, for the first time in his life he looked at Cheryl in an entirely new light. Instead of just appraising her as "girlfriend" material, Randy got the sense that Cheryl was a woman who was going somewhere, with or without him. She had pushed one of the key **Marriage Motivator** buttons. Her stock was high and there were other takers. He wasn't threatened by Cheryl's tough questions but rather impressed with her strength, and as a result their romance deepened. They each felt lucky to have the other in their lives.

So what happened the next time they went out to their favorite Greek restaurant? This time Randy brought up the subject of marriage and kids. "That's what you really want, huh?" Randy asked.

Cheryl smiled, knowing her maneuvering had worked in her favor, and answered, "Of course. I mean, I'm not afraid to admit there are certain things in life I want to experience."

They ordered another bottle of Greek wine and went home arm in arm, experiencing the joyful rush of, well, Marriage Momentum.

WHAT WE HAVE LEARNED: While you may think that our use of the word *maneuvering* indicates that we're advocating subterfuge, we're not—we don't condone game playing in any way (unless it's Pictionary). However, Marriage Maneuvering does consist of some artful and graceful shifting. Marriage Maneuvering generally refers to your understated behavior in the crucial time period between your decision that you've found your future husband and his decision that the feeling's mutual. While playing it cool and hanging out is fully encouraged for a deliriously happy and stress-free period of time, it's never a bad idea to put out relationship-based feelers to find out where he stands. Once you've done this, you will then know what strategy to follow in order to take the relationship the full distance. Remember: Marriage Maneuvering is *not* a game or a series of tricks. It's about getting through the tipping point to your relationship at which a small, subtle hint or change on your part can create a significant shift that creates Marriage Momentum.

As Cheryl and Randy are an abstract example, we're going to give you concrete pointers to help you jump-start your Marriage Momentum. We are going to train you to recognize the strengths you possess that will trounce his resistance to marriage. Since you've got to get him to think that marriage will be as wonderful as *you* think it will be, we've created a comprehensive list of what we call **Marriage Motivators** that will help you prevail over any emotional barriers he's put up to stop you.

Many of our married male friends who were *not* initially inclined to get married referenced one or more of the Marriage Motivators listed below as being influential in pushing them toward the altar. Read them. Memorize them. Post them on thy fridge— just not where he can see them. We don't recommend crudely rattling them off or even talking about them. Remember, understanding which marriage motivators will work means you understand what makes your Target Audience tick, something you should not be inclined to reveal. These are strategic touch points; once you understand them, the most successful plan is to use them genuinely and subtly.

Marriage Motivators

Motivator 1: WINNING THE PRIZE

Most men are competitive. From income, to cars, to sports, to the locker room shower, competing for women is no different. We're not *suggesting* that men objectify you as a material thing. We're *telling* you that they do.

There is a certain amount of bragging rights attached to snagging one's dream girl. When a man has also taken a girl off the market *and* believes that he has done so at the expense of other men, it is that much sweeter.

What you can do: It's always important to give him the impression that, like a stock, you're selling high. You need to let him know that out in the marriage market there's a market for *you* and there is no shortage of takers out there. An old saying your grandmother may have repeated to you is "Run after a man until he thinks he's caught you." Listen to your grandma. (Hey, figure that *your* mother didn't listen to her mother and *you* didn't listen to yours, so Grandma's advice must be good for you.)

Motivator 2: MEN WANT MAMA

Inside every tough guy is that little boy who wants to be comforted, babied, and healed. Let's not forget that man's first position was hanging off a breast. For some men, things haven't changed all that much.

What you can do: At every stage of your relationship it's important to demonstrate that no matter how long you two are together, you will continue to care for him. While most women don't sign up for the Man = Baby deal, the ability to nurture her man is a crucial trait for the artful deal closer. If you're unconditionally supportive and loyal, whether it's with his friends, family, or coworkers, Mr. Right won't be willing to give up your compassion so quickly. Furthermore, an intuitive woman knows how to transition from the "babying" stage to the "seduction" phase smoothly enough that her man never notices (or gets diaper rash). If you haven't perfected this, it's all about giving him just the right amount of attention.

Motivator 3:
WHAT'S A BLOW JOB BETWEEN FRIENDS?

This is about two of the most important things you can offer your man: friendship and sexin'. As much as men seek male bonding, we also seek many of the same traits in our wives as we do in our buddies, namely loyalty, intelligence, and a consistent topspin forehand. But the one thing men don't seek from their best buds—well, at least the ones that you won't find constructing the Y in YMCA—is the hot stuff. Therefore, finding a best friend, tennis partner, copilot, and confidante with whom he can do the nasty is a big perk.

What you can do: Be one of the boys but with extra benefits by letting him know that once in a while you're willing to do or talk about anything, including some "guy" things. For example, the next time he's watching a baseball game and his buddy George is out of town, offer to keep him company while he watches the game. Then let him get to third base on *you*—or vice versa. Let's hope he thinks baseball with George was never this good.

Motivator 4: INSTANT RESPECTABILITY!

Even if he was once arrested for exposing himself in public, once a man gets hitched, it confirms *instant* respectability in almost every community. Besides talking about the wife around the water cooler or being able to go on a double date with the boss and his wife, it's a powerful thing when a man can speak for two.

What you can do: Even if he still plays video games and laughs at the sound of his own farts, the world often treats married people with a higher level of respect. Need proof? On average, married men make more money than single men the same age (source: *Current Population Survey 2000*). Marriage, for some men, can be a huge boost of confidence—and men love nothing more than being proud and having someone be proud and protective of them. (We'll see this demonstrated later with a couple we love.)

Motivator 5: TWO FOR THE PRICE OF ONE

If corporations have figured out one thing in recent decades, besides how to misstate earnings, it is that the right merger or acquisition can create a true synergy. Many men (and women) are worried about their economic futures, and the thought of a wife and family can bring up huge issues of fear, doubt, and self-loathing (and some use this as an excuse for not being ready). Besides greater earning power, some men might like the idea of having a *financial partner.* This can give a sense of relief to many men, even if it's for something as simple as having someone who can fill out the annual income tax form (or send his W2s to the accountant).

What you can do: Allay this fear and you can reap huge rewards. Demonstrating that you have the same values and monetary goals will prove to him that together you can be an economic force. Whether it's the idea of dual incomes paying for one domicile or crunching numbers together to plan for a house, many men we know love having a financial sounding board in the family. You also need to make him feel—and vice versa—that you are mentally and *fiscally* of sound mind. This doesn't mean you should start coupon clipping if you're not doing that already. It does mean that finances are a *huge* issue for most men when they consider marriage, so showing that you'll be an asset rather than a liability will pay huge dividends in the future.

Motivator 6: DIPPING MY WICK CAN MAKE ME SICK

This one's fairly self-explanatory. The consequences of running around with too many partners can catch up to anyone. Truthfully, we don't think the fear of a scourge has closed that many deals, but if a man thinks that the future long-term happiness of his willy is at stake, he may start to reevaluate his lifestyle and prefer monogamy.

What you can do: If you don't know the definite statistics

of sexually transmitted diseases, just make them up. He'll never know. Either way, HIV/AIDS and all the others really suck (to put it mildly). Gently remind him that outside of abstinence, the best insurance policy against sexually transmitted diseases is monogamy.

Motivator 7: WHERE'S MY GIFT WITH PURCHASE?
Whether it's social, financial, or culinary, sharing the family wealth or traditions is another way to help close the deal. Someone in the family must have some drool-eliciting asset like courtside Lakers tickets, a country club membership, or a business to go into? A free gift with purchase is one of the most successful tools used to bring in customers—just look at McDonald's Happy Meals. A perk is a perk, and that can perk up any deal; in marketing lingo, a perk encourages *acquisition*. It doesn't hurt if your last name is Hearst, but anything big or small can make a deal more attractive. As long as the perk isn't the *main reason* he's with you, there no reason to think this is a negative. It's just part of what makes you unique!

What you can do: Should you have neither a famous name nor a spread in Palm Beach, not to fret. Since the beginning of time, this so-called dowry principle can be applied to anything *extra* he thinks he's getting by way of the deal. While neither of us got married for that antique silver service set or the time-share in Boca, for one of us, it certainly helped the cause knowing that our wife's grandmother had great genes and looked twenty years younger than her age. Depending on what your man is into, the perk could mean anything as simple as the best barbecue sauce from Mom, the finest free legal work from Dad, or stock tips from your sis.

Motivator 8: HOW CAN I CHANGE PAMPERS IF I'M WEARING DEPENDS?

Many men want to get a few things out of their system when they're young, vibrant, and virile. Yet, even the world's biggest sex symbols eventually get "played out." Sure they're good at bedding and not wedding, but a seventy-year-old Lothario is about as sexy as ass dimples. Age has a lot to do with men succumbing to bended-knee gravity, so whether it's arthritis or a good career move, men shouldn't be having kids when they're as much in need as a toddler for diapers.

What you can do: There are plenty of ways you can subtly remind him that he's not getting any younger. For example, at his next birthday, put *all* thirty-six candles on his cake. That should light a fire under his ass.

Motivator 9: I WANT TO SPREAD MY SEED

It's a natural evolutionary fact: we want to spread our semen like dogs want to spread their scent. While you don't have to be hitched to start a family, if having kids in wedlock is a goal, responsible people usually make a commitment to each other at some point, at least for the benefit of the children. We both feel that we were put on this earth to be fathers, and marriage was one step closer to that goal. (Though procreation wasn't the first thing on our Why We Wed list).

What you can do: While this Motivator should be discussed later in the relationship, it's a very potent tool. Realizing that if he plays his cards right he could be coaching Little League and having twenty little ones hanging on his every word will speak volumes to his inner father. Just don't bring it up on the first few dates.

Motivator 10: LOVE (WE SAVED THE BEST FOR LAST)

No, it's not a fable. Most men do marry for love. Having one's heartstrings pulled in the midst of a fun, loving, sexy, and compatible relationship is still the best reason to close the deal. If he loves you and doesn't want to lose you, he'll do the right thing. Love isn't old-fashioned. Love isn't fiction or the residue of a Lifetime drama. His love for you is and always will be the number-one reason he'll want to close the deal.

What you can do: Love him.

WITH THESE BASIC Marriage Motivators outlined for you, you now understand some fundamental ideas that induce men to pop the question.

Marketing Marriage

IN THE DAYS OF ARRANGED MARRIAGES (OF royal families for diplomacy's sake or religious families for G-d's sake), the patriarch or village matchmaker was the primitive form of marketer and closer in this deal-making process. Through perfected presentation skills, the matchmaker was most likely able to minimize her client's flaws and maximize her attributes. Imagine a European description 250 years ago: "She's beautiful (read: she has two limbs intact), petite, and curvy (read: she's short but can still bear children), from the Minsk suburbs (read: she's not overly sophisticated but she's not a hick either), and I needn't tell you her father has a very successful timber business (read: she's so loaded you won't mind that she's got wooden teeth)."

These days, matchmakers only *find* you men and can't guarantee a proposal, so if you want to nail your catch you will have to do some of the marriage marketing yourself. After all, nobody other than your parents wants marriage and kids for you more than you do. So you'll have to learn how to sell yourself without coming off as a Salad Shooter infomercial. Let's go over a few things to help you make the sale to your male.

Whether we're marketing soft drinks or soft porn, we're here to beat those marketing skills into your *subconscious*. All the more reason to take into account the following.

Your Asset Guide

WHILE SIMILAR TO OUR LIST OF MARRIAGE Motivators in that it's an insight into what men think, this list refers not to what will motivate him toward marriage but to ways that you can creatively market yourself—and the idea of marriage to him. In the advertising or marketing world, one of these assets would be called the USP, or unique selling proposition, and in Hollywood it's called the hook. We call it your **Asset Guide.** Just remember: It's all about the spin, so think positively!

Family

Some people love marrying into a big, festive family to come home to during the holidays. If this sounds like your partner, and you have a great relationship with your family, offer it up! Sleepovers for Christmas and New Year's, playing touch football in the yard with the bros-in-law, always having couples to vacation with, family reunions and name tags! Give him a taste but let him know that things get better when his name is yours too.

Net: Many guys want to marry into a big, social family (read: their own personal sports team). Visit the Kennedy compound in Hyannisport for pointers.

What Family?

You hardly have any relationship with your family. Plenty of guys (not us—we love our families) don't want the hassle. Some are not interested in attending your nephew's christening or Little League games and can't stand giving up weekends for picnics with the future mother-in-law. If he's not down with family events and neither are you, tell him that you prefer to travel light—you've got no baggage.

Net: If having little or no family obligations is very appealing to your boyfriend and you're of the same mind, then take advantage of the holidays. Use those days off from work to get some bonus alone time.

Lifestyle (or Helping Him Get a Life)

So many of the women we know lead interesting lives filled with fabulous jobs, great friends, and many interests, and many of the men we spoke to were easily prone to boredom, falling into routines and in need of direction and a social life. When a man becomes deeply integrated in your life, very often the thought of losing you and everything you offer becomes as scary as your prom photos. Whether you work as a music producer or an administrative assistant, every man loves it if his social life's expanded. Take him out to that rock concert or a Christmas party. Flaunt a new social life of activities that will make his head spin. A great circle of friends and a fun lifestyle is addictive. Only you have the power to make him an addict. And when it comes to your friends, don't forget to ask for that upgrade we mentioned in Motivator 7. Does a family member have a condo in the Caymans? A palace in Paris? There's nothing like being able to hotel (v.) properties for your own use. And it doesn't have to be family property either. Did your old roommate move to Hawaii? Now she can repay you for all those nights you held her hair as she kneeled in front of the sorority toilet. Don't be afraid to ask anyone for payback in creating a great lifestyle when it's deal-closing time.

Net: No woman wants a man who is solely interested in material things or exclusive social plans; however, your ability to expand his social life and keep it interesting will have a direct impact on your relationship.

Genetics: She's Not Heavy, She's My Mother

Is someone, anyone, in the family interesting? Is there even a dark sheep? Sure, it's nice to say that your grandpappy was a Supreme Court judge, but don't be ashamed if your great-grandmother was a madam in the Old West. Colorful can be fun, sexy, and exciting, so shake what your momma gave you! Make your gene pool look Olympic even if it's shallower than a Hollywood marriage.

Is your mother (or a close female relative) great-looking? Does she have a distinctive feature—for example, big brown eyes or a great body or maybe even body parts (legs, hands, or a smile will do)? Even if you aren't blessed with the ability to say, "Look at my mom—see how great she looks at [insert age here]?" which infers you will too, find something. If your mother weighs in at 290, tell him how she goes up a bra size every few years.

Net: Everyone has been blessed with something special, from height, to a smile, to a great personality. Play it up, not down.

Spending Time with the Osbournes

Be careful with whom you hang, as your decisions may hang you. You should take charge of your environment. Surround yourself with FUN, happily married couples and weed out *overly satisfied* singles. Lose people in your life who must talk about their recent ménage à trois with sexy flight attendants. There's no sense in getting your man daydreaming when he should be deal closing.

Also, many a deal has failed because an ex–love interest enters the equation and unnecessarily complicates things. If you haven't yet cut loose your FBC (former booty call), now's obviously the time. FBCs don't really want *you;* they want the *idea* of you around to keep their options open. If you've made up your mind that your current man is the end game, then having your FBC around only makes for trouble. These deals can be as fragile as your man's ego.

Net: Monitor your social circle and make sure you're hanging with people who don't undermine the institution of marriage. In other words, keep the exes and randy single pals to a minimum.

Lobby for a Mutual Hobby

Before you have a hubby, sometimes you need to find a hobby. Whether it's travel, skiing, cooking, or shopping, find something you two love to do together. This can also mean exploring new things—from botany classes at the Brooklyn Botanical Gardens to Botox injection parties in Beverly Hills. Every couple should try to keep it captivating and communal.

Too many couples just rely on a standing Saturday-night time slot and assume that this is maximum effort, but if you want a sexy and solid relationship, both of you must invest time and thought into creating an exciting backdrop for your courtship. While the idea of "getting" a hobby may sound trite, look at the things you enjoy together as a couple. It can be as simple as going to the movies together, cooking, or miniature golf. The important thing is that you are always having fun *together.*

Net: Couples that play together, stay together. Of course, we're not advocating that you spend *all* your time together, but if you're getting together only for a meal, sex, or shopping, while that's nice, it's not a relationship.

Getting Maid

It's called homemaking, and it's not a four-letter word. No, it's not just for women anymore, but if you think your man is focused on clean living, you may want to think again. We're not suggesting you must take a step backward in gender evolution and vacuum his apartment and do his laundry, but let's face it, everyone (you included) needs a little service; the *least* you can do is put a bagel on the table on a Sunday morning.

What we're really talking about here are those little endearments that demonstrate "I really care about you." If you're waiting for him to do something like this first and no one does it, then you will find yourself in a "fend for yourself" relationship, and that's not a good place to be. If your man loves to cook and serve you, lucky you (at least offer to help clean up). If he doesn't and you still don't want to cook, no one is saying you should. Setting a lovely table and ordering in will do just fine. He'll feel the strength of this asset if you make sure he has his favorite beer or ice cream. Most men want to feel like they're the king of the castle. Really.

Net: Being independent, powerful, and an equal partner in a relationship is wonderful, but that's not what we're talking about here. We think you should be demonstrative and partnering in creating a pleasurable home life, even if you're not technically living there, yet. Hopefully, he'll be doing the same for you.

Sibling or Sybil

Your bro or sis can aid or abet in the deal-closing process, so be aware of what the family might say. Can you see your brother turning to your man, slapping him on the back, and saying "Can't wait for you to take little Sis off our hands. Mom and Dad have been dealing with all her psycho shit for years. Does your health plan at work cover behavioral therapy?" If so, then maybe you should keep him at bay for the time being.

On the other hand, if your siblings are your best public relations advocates, then make sure they have ample opportunity to sing your praises in front of your man. For example, if you can imagine your brother saying, "Hey, Sis, remember when the Dallas Cowboys cheerleaders tried to recruit you at your Mensa reunion?" then invite your big brother over to the apartment more often. That should make an impression.

Net: For many of us, our first real relationships (outside that with the 'rents) were with a brother or sister. While no one is saying you have to be close or even get along, it certainly speaks volumes for you if you do and if your siblings say only positive things (or at least hold back the truth). Third-party credibility is always a great plus in having your man get to know and respect you.

WHILE WE MAY NOT HAVE LISTED every Marriage Motivator or highlighted every possible relationship Asset out there, we hope we were able to get you attuned to the kinds of things your man is thinking about or concentrating on and what *you* can be doing. Some of you may be wondering why you are supposed to be doing all the work. If your man is making little or no effort, that's not a good sign. But if he responds positively to some of the aforementioned stimuli, then keep going—your proficiency in CRM (couple relationship management) will pay off in no time.

Information Overload

THOUGH THIS ISN'T NEUROSCIENCE OR A graduate course in marketing, it's important that you digest the specifics of this chapter. Marketing marriage and yourself isn't fun, but it's in some ways a necessary evil. Like big business, it's hard work and requires practiced finesse. After all, in the world of direct marketing, the main buzzwords are *acquisition* and *retention*, and if they don't relate to closing the deal, we don't know what does.

Finally, a few words of caution: If you're transparently obviously about what we have just been discussing here or are not sincere in your efforts, it can work against you. No man would rather hear textbook speak over honest conversation. Seeming too eager can scare him off, and if you're totally nonchalant about it, your clueless mate will be sure to miss the message. So start slowly, try out a few motivators, and see what happens. Once you integrate into your life or conversation some of the tips from this chapter, they will become second nature and you may find your relationship has entered an entirely new level of understanding.

3 The Princess and the Pee

A COUPLE WHO HAD BEEN DATING FOR A
few months started to do the sleepover thing. At the time, it wasn't
that casual but it really wasn't that serious either. The guy had
been most surprised about how comfortable and uncomplicated
the relationship was. It didn't hurt that when he looked over at the
girl first thing in the morning, he admired her sexy repose and
natural beauty. Little did he know that she obsessively got out of
bed a half hour earlier than the alarm, crept into the bathroom,
brushed her hair and teeth, and crawled back into bed like a CIA
operative, only to "wake up" in his arms looking and smelling like
sunshine. You think that would never happen? Sure it would. It
happened to one of us.

Now before you say that *you* would never do this because it
isn't an honest portrayal of who you really are, need we remind
you of something called makeup? Ah, you say, and what about
your reeking breath, smelly underarms, and stubbly chin? Why
aren't *you* stealing off and presenting yourself in the best possible
light first thing in the morning? That's not such a bad idea. Nobody wants a hag or a hobo by his or her side first thing when
the alarm goes off. But unless you're the one who's planning on
popping the question, we suggest you start the hygiene process
yourself. Maybe he'll catch on.

One of the benefits of modern society is that men and women
have the opportunity to peek under the covers in a relationship

before they make a true commitment, whether it's a casual sleep-over or a decision to live together. What men are exposed to can often affect their desire to close the deal. What we're going to tackle in this chapter is how to *control* what men see. Clearly not all men want to see the same things, but generally men want what personifies the female gender. In other words, men seek every-thing that they're not, and that's what you need to give them.

We Want You!

WE'VE MENTIONED THIS BEFORE: MEN LOVE how soft and feminine women can be. We love how striking you can look, whether you're dressing up for dinner with friends or wearing our boxers for breakfast on Sunday morning. It's not just about how you look and smell, though. For the record, for the most part, we like women who don't act like men.

What man wouldn't want to come home to a warm, caring, and sweet demeanor? It's a hard world out there, and a little mental and physical softness can go a long way.

Before you get the wrong idea, however, we think it's great to misbehave in certain circumstances. At the racetrack, at a ball game, or even at work, women who can dish it out can be a source of great fun. Sure, there are lots of men who love to hang with a girl because she's just like one of the guys. Chances are they even want a little nookie from her, but that doesn't mean they're con-templating any sort of deal closing. In the majority of social set-tings and in intimate surroundings, crudeness is not an asset.

Intimate Impressions; or, What Do the Words *Groom* and *Grooming* Have in Common?

YOU'VE OFTEN HEARD PEOPLE TALK AT length about first impressions and how important they are, but what about impressions in the *intimate* sense? How well groomed you are may answer more questions about you than five dinner dates: Do you smell? Do you wear granny underwear or sexy thongs? Do you sleep in lingerie or sweatpants? Do you shave and moisturize your legs every day or every leap year?

Men are idealistic when it comes to women. They really *do* want to put their woman on a pedestal. Understand, though, that with many men there are only two categories: (1) a pedestal and (2) a surface to rest his beer can on. Giving 100 percent effort in the grooming department is never wasted on a future groom.

Once you dive under the covers, the intimate impression can enhance or derail any romance. For example, these days not a lot of men are hunters and they don't seek out the heavy bush. If you don't know what your boyfriend prefers and you are indifferent about your bikini wax, find out how he likes you styled. More and more, personal grooming choices seem to go in and out of fashion like hemlines. One week it's the "landing strip," the next it's "Brazilian," and the following it's bare down there. Most guys we've spoken to do have a preference as to how they like their girlfriends styled. Whatever you decide, don't forget that neatness counts for 10 percent of your grade.

Aside from personal hygiene and style, getting to a more intimate place can mean many things, including sharing personal spaces. While no man should ever object to making room in his medicine cabinet for female products, there is a difference between arranging for space on a glass shelf and seeing used 'pons floating around in the toilet: Just because you're used to it doesn't mean he is.

While some of these may seem obvious to you, our wives tell

us that public women's rooms are totally disgusting, so there must be some truth to our worries. We've been lucky ourselves and haven't experienced any nastiness, but we can't say the same for Ian, a friend of ours. After dating a girl for three months, he told us that he accidentally barged in on his girlfriend biting a hangnail. Which didn't sound so bad to us at first, until he told us it was on her toe. *Classy.* Getting intimate is wonderful, but do know that if you want him to treat your body like a temple, make sure it doesn't look like a house of *whore*ship.

It's not as if men don't need to take care of themselves as well, but let's face it, the cultural (double) standards for hygiene and grooming are somewhat lower for men. Most men think nothing of washing their hands and toweling off their face after a ten-mile run and then sitting down to a romantic dinner. If you feel your lover has potential but tends to smell potent, then you have to be honest about what turns you on or off. Intimacy goes both ways, and certainly life's most intimate acts are fair game for both sexes in creating a happy relationship.

The Groom in the Bath and Bedroom Quiz

ARE YOU MISBEHAVING IN INTIMATE SITUATIONS? Getting close to your boyfriend will assuredly include moments that are extremely private, and how you handle them can make the difference in appearing like a lady or a tramp. As one of our wives tells us, "There are some things that should be permanently left to your imagination." Let's see what you'd do:

1. You get to his apartment and you really have to go to the bathroom.
   a. You leave the door open and continue your conversation.
   b. You tell him to put on a video. You're going to be a while.

c. You discreetly excuse yourself and spray on some perfume (or light a match) before exiting the loo.

d. You tell him you're glad you got there just in time, as you were about to poo in your pants.

Answer: *c*. Discreetly excuse yourself.

While bodily functions are natural and normal, how you handle them, especially in a studio apartment, is crucial to setting the level of respect in your relationship. A spritz of your favorite perfume (that you keep in your handbag for just such an occasion) should do the trick, as Murphy's Law dictates that your man is always bound to enter the bathroom almost immediately after you.

2. How did you decide which side of the bed you slept on last night at his apartment?

   a. You dug your nails into his back and pushed him onto the wet spot.

   b. You observed where he naturally put his watch or alarm clock and decided you would deal with the opposite side.

   c. You picked the side nearest the kitchen, which allowed you to quietly get up and make him breakfast in bed in the morning.

   d. You suggested you sleep diagonally because everything had to be equal.

Answer: *b*. How you negotiate your sleeping arrangements at his place is a sign of how you respect his authority and his house rules. While bed-related homicides are not a major concern to most police departments, bad diplomacy here can set a terrible precedent. Take it from us: You will probably continue to negotiate over blankets, pillows, room temperature, and sleeping positions throughout the rest of your courtship and well into marriage, so handle your bediquette with diplomacy that will stand the test of time. And one last thing: Making him bagels and lox in bed sounds great, but if you try this too early and unless you plan on doing it often, he may think it smells a little fishy.

3. **Where do you put your clothes before you hit the hay?**
   a. You leave them on the floor.
   b. You push aside his suits and take a bar in his closet
   c. You fold them up hobo style in a bundle and sleep on them, like a pillow.
   d. You pick up a few things and casually throw them over the side of a chair.

   Answer: *d.* You pick up a few things and casually throw them over the side of a chair.

   Nonchalantly draping garments over a chair suggests a casual elegance and respect for your things while not giving away an uptight or obsessive vibe. Men are usually slobs, save for the "Felix" strain (you know, the anal-retentive organizer who probably alphabetizes his cereal boxes).* The addition of female items and paraphernalia can be a shock to the male system and, for more reasons than one, hopefully your man isn't used to multiple thongs lying around his bedroom.

4. **You're having sex and the phone rings.**
   a. You let the machine get it.
   b. You grab the phone and answer it with a resounding, "YES?! YES?!"
   c. You check the caller ID and decide whether to pick it up.
   d. You answer it because it's your client, handle whatever it is quickly, and pick up where you left off.

   Answer: *a.* Let the machine get it.

----

* This is a reference to *The Odd Couple* for those of you under thirty.

Interrupting an intimate moment to answer the telephone is rude and insulting and can build up resentment like almost nothing else can. Keep the intimate moments intimate by staying focused and involved. Your stopping in the middle of sex (or even an important conversation) to handle less important business will no doubt make your partner feel inadequate—and make him wonder why he can't hold your attention or why he isn't a priority. Unless a life is in danger, don't stop for nothin'.

5. You're not on birth control, neither of you wants a kid out of wedlock, and you want to use a condom but he hates them. What do you say?

   a. Damn, this happens to me all the time!
   b. That's fine, if you'll just sign my prenegotiated child support agreement here and here.
   c. No problem—you look like you're HIV negative.
   d. Sorry, it's safe sex or no sex.

   Answer: *d*. Sorry, it's safe sex or no sex.

   Ladies, there should be no compromise on this issue—there's too much at stake for you. When you go skin to skin, don't be shy about demanding whatever protection you want and deserve. If he gets too angry and tries to talk you out of it, take that as a sign. Believe it or not, most men we know would forgo the pleasures of sex *sans* latex if they knew their other choice would be an unwanted pregnancy. If and when you decide to have intercourse, make sure your partner provides you with a clean bill of health. Until then, a (latex) condom can be the best form of available life insurance.

6. You wake up and need your doughnut and coffee.

   a. You nudge him and then tell him to make like Spot and fetch.

b. You hunt around the kitchen for some coffee or tea and put the kettle on for both.

c. You scavenge the icebox and scarf down his last piece of crumb cake.

d. You bitch-slap him because all that he has in his kitchen are condoms and condiments.

Answer: *b.* hunt around the kitchen for some coffee or tea and put the kettle on for both.

A simple gesture like putting the kettle on and taking out two cups can seem like a breath of fresh air to a man. After all, most single men aren't used to pampering, so this may feel like five-star service. It also says that you have a nurturing side, which is important to guys who are looking for a potential mate.

7. *Your boyfriend gets home while you're on the phone with your best friend.*

a. You wrap up the call quickly and tell her you'll call her back later.

b. You kiss him and continue talking.

c. You go to the bathroom with the cordless before he sees you and tell him that you've got a bad tummy-ache.

d. You give him a warm greeting while you're on the phone and wait to see if he needs you before you get off.

Answer: *a.* wrap up the call quickly and tell her you'll call her back later.

You may think that *d* is also an appropriate answer, but it's not. Making your man feel like the Man of the House is crucial to closing the deal, and showing him that nothing comes before him will help him feel that way. When your boss walks by your desk, do you see if he or she needs you before you stop trolling eBay for that perfect handbag? Of course not. Same logic applies here. When your boyfriend walks in your door, your world should revolve around him (and vice versa).

As the saying goes, most men unconsciously or consciously marry their mothers, so they look for women who embody the traits that they have come to believe are quintessential. When boyfriends take their girlfriends home to their families, they're usually seeking approval from the people whose opinions they trust and whose qualities they hold dear. However, the families can't see under your covers; he'll be the only one who makes any serious decisions based on that. While hygiene isn't a problem in all relationships, when it is, it can be a major issue. Take Marnie, for example.

Marnie

MARNIE HAS IT ALL. She's gorgeous (really), tawny skinned, and has the coolest loft (flat-screen TV over the fireplace). Marnie is hilarious, smart as a whip, and has buckets of cash (Daddy's a big-time lawyer). Plus, she dresses like she's on *Sex and the City* and looks great in a bikini. So how come the girl who has it all has no one? After speaking to a few of her exes (we know them), we found out that Marnie needs to clean up her act, and we mean literally. Including her potty mouth (though it was funny in college).

Marnie curses like a drunken sailor, and her idea of a shower is a spritz of perfume. In addition, her nails are always dirty and she has a ring around her collar (and one of us had a grandmother who always said you can never trust a girl with a dirty neck). Marnie's awesome, spacious loft is one big Dumpster for dirty laundry, dishes, and ashtrays. She has the "sorority sister gone bad" persona of one who loves doing Jell-O shots and thinks disgusting table manners are funny as well (she's been known to burp up her Mexican food at the dinner table). Marnie's the life of the party and always stands out in a crowd, but her lack of hygiene and manners has been the death of several serious relationships.

When Marnie turned twenty-seven she was serious with a banker named Cal. Marnie loved that Cal was close with his family and often talked about how he wanted a family of his own in the near future. Cal was crazy about Marnie and loved her zany, brilliant sense of humor and her love of sports. He found her incredibly sexy and thought she was adventurous both in and out of bed, which is why he overlooked most of her hygiene issues for a while.

At first Cal figured Marnie was probably just too busy at work to get around to cleaning her apartment. Cal wasn't exactly a neat freak either, so initially he was quite happy that his girlfriend was cool about it when he left his dirty dishes in her sink. However, over the next few months, Cal realized that the real reason for Marnie's dirty ways wasn't Marnie's busy schedule; she was just a natural slob. Things took a turn for the worse one Sunday morning when Cal sat down on the couch to watch football on the plasma and found a moldy Chinese food container under one of the cushions. Marnie quickly apologized and threw it into one of the three open garbage bags in the kitchen. Cal told her that in his four years in a fraternity, he'd never seen someone lose a food container in a couch. (Marnie found that hard to believe.) The more difficult thing to swallow, Cal told us later, was that with all the other odors in that apartment, he hadn't even smelled the festering food.

A few weeks later, Marnie and Cal made plans for dinner with another couple, Joel and Tara. Marnie loved hanging around other young married couples because afterward Cal would often remark that he couldn't wait to be the official Man of the House. Marnie also knew that Joel and Tara liked hanging out with her because her sick sense of humor always made them laugh.

The evening of the dinner, Marnie got home late from work and grabbed a dress from the pile on her chair, threw on her jacket, and was out the door. When she arrived at the restaurant, Cal, Joel, and Tara were waiting for her at the table and Cal got up to take her jacket. That's when everyone noticed the big red stain on her dress. Marnie rolled her eyes and made light of it: "This is what you get when you get dressed in the dark. I thought I sent this dress to the cleaner after I spilled wine—" Tara interrupted her. "At our house three months ago?" Marnie laughed. "Yes! How funny is that?" Needless to say, nobody thought it was *that* funny. Cal was pretty embarrassed and started looking at Marnie with new, clearer eyes.

Soon, Cal no longer found the hair in the tub endearing or her general untidiness a sweet character flaw. Marnie gave a whole new meaning to a girl who was dirty in bed. One night, after Marnie sneezed over Cal's entrée at dinner (no kidding), Cal pretty much decided he'd had enough. He'd casually confronted her about cleaning up her act before, but now he was serious. She grew up in a nice home. Why was this so difficult?

Marnie was surprised at first and couldn't believe that Cal was really so upset by her behavior. "Since when are you so uptight about this stuff?" she asked Cal. Cal responded, "Since I started thinking about how you were going to raise our kids." Marnie really didn't know what to say to that one.

Things didn't change much over the next few months, so her cleanliness became the main issue whenever they fought. Cal gradually stopped going over to Marnie's apartment and eventually they were seeing each other only one night a week. Cal finally called it quits when he realized that Marnie was making no effort to change her ways, which he took as a reflection of her feelings for him. Perhaps Marnie's philosophy of "love me for who I am" has some merit, but if you are in need of a good scrub-down, you may need to stop and smell the perspiration.

Is the Marnie example extreme? Maybe. Lately, however, we have observed some pretty nasty habits that won't help in any deal closing. Whether it's talking on cell phones during dinners, not making efforts to look their best for each other, or speaking to each other disrespectfully in public, bad manners erode the basic foundations of relationships. The same goes for bad grooming and uncleanliness—they all make the statement that you don't have the greatest respect for your partner or yourself. Or you aren't willing to do the work.

Are you still not sure that you'd pass the test for even the most basic hygiene and manners requirements for marriage? We've made it easier than ever to find out.

The Definitive No-Nos for Dummies List

THE FINAL STEP IN THE SELF-EXAMINATION of your personal habits is to review a definitive list of intimate faux pas. This is the ultimate list of No-Nos standing between you and your Yes! Yes!

1. Unwanted facial hair (bleaching is for underwear).
2. Underarm hair (unless you're from Latvia).
3. A lot of makeup (unless you're a clown or dating one).
4. Cursing like a drunken sailor especially after belching, farting, or throwing up (unless you're Courtney Love).
5. Eating more at the buffet than your man (unless you're with child).
6. Gnarly toenails and dirty bitten-down nails (unless you're a grape stomper, a potter, or a ranch hand).
7. Breath that smells like fish or an ashtray (unless you're a mermaid or a jazz singer).
8. Unwashed private parts (unless you're spayed).
9. Green teeth (unless you're British).
10. Hairy moles (unless you're Cindy Crawford).

Make Efforts, Not Ef*farts*

MEN WANT A WOMAN WHO KNOWS NOT ONLY what the word *clean* means but also what the word *maintenance* means—and you know we're not talking janitorial services. Getting him hooked on your hygiene only to let yourself go later is not going to help close the deal either. Sustained effort and commitment to your appearance, hygiene, and good behavior are going to pay dividends throughout your relationship and beyond . . . so don't be lazy.

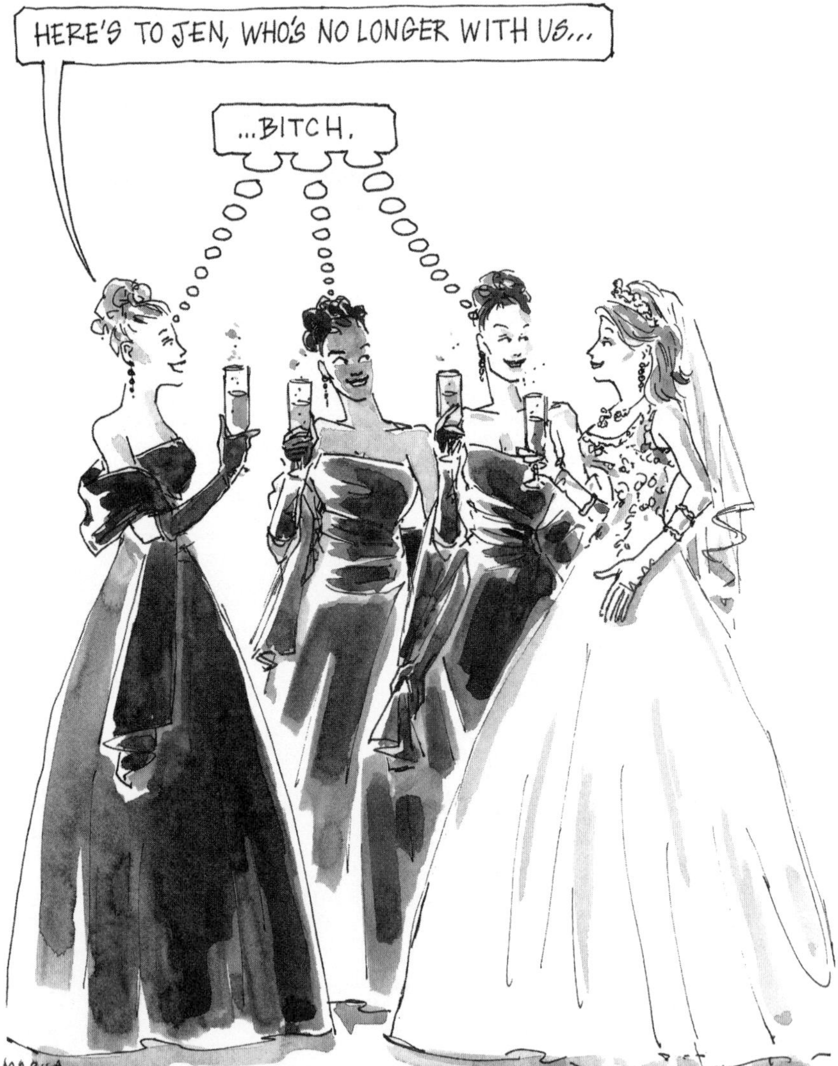
HERE'S TO JEN, WHO'S NO LONGER WITH US...
...BITCH.
MARISA MARCHETTO

4

What's She Got That I Haven't Got? How About a Man?

FAT (WITH AN F) FELICIA AND THAT HO Shawn can do it—they can close deals—and you can't. And no matter how much you spend getting a new haircut or buying another pair of bank-breaking shoes, other women are closing the deal while you dawdle in despair. For the record, ladies, most guys can't tell the difference between Prada and Payless. And if they *can* . . .

In this chapter, we'll discuss how you can easily separate yourself from the competition without spending a small fortune. You knew how to attract your boyfriend's attention in the first place, but now we believe you should hear some of the finer points on keeping it that way *forever.* Marriage and commitment are tough, and you'd be smart to wonder how you, while swimming in the vast sea of available women, can keep him by your side and interested for the rest of his life. Our philosophy, you will see, is quite simple, but it has managed to escape the rules of engagement of many women.

The *Closing the Deal* Philosophy on Competition

EVEN IF YOUR LAST NAME STARTS WITH AN *O* and ends with a *nassis* you may have some concern that other single women have the potential to come between your boyfriend and the ultimate commitment. Yes, there *are* gorgeous single women everywhere (in fact, on a recent trip to Brazil one of the authors learned that in Sao Paulo, women outnumber men seven to one), but by the end of this chapter that's not going to bother you at all. You see, we are going to show you the foolproof way to guarantee that you will *never* lose a competition again! That's right! How? Easy: *You're going to agree to a noncompete clause.*

Competition has no place in the act of courting, unless you're talking tennis. We think it's important that you go through life knowing that your future husband is interested in how great you are, *not* how great you compare to the standard deviation from the mean of all great women.

We don't care if you are surrounded by the most beautiful women on the planet on a daily basis. If you refuse to compete with these women, then by definition there *is no* competition. As we've said earlier and will repeat again, self-confidence in a woman is an incredibly attractive character trait to most men (who are worth marrying anyway), and no self-respecting, self-confident women would ever feel the need to engage in covert or overt competition with other women. It is beneath them.

Historically, when it comes to the dating and marriage arena, women are not other women's best allies. Competition often brings out the worst qualities in people, and in the world of dating, competition can cause women (and men) to exhibit some ugly behavior. This conduct can be a major turnoff for men, whether men are consciously aware of it or not. That's not to say that men don't enjoy a good catfight once in a while. But generally, if you're overly negative for seemingly no-good or nonexistent reasons, men are going to sense it and be turned off by it.

It's not just your behavior that's an issue, but others'. Being around negative women can cause you to undermine yourself and thus irreparably harm your ability to close the deal. When you're in a relationship, the important thing is focusing your energy on your relationship, not on other women. While you can't control how other women behave, you can control how you react to it.

Playa hataz,* as the name suggests, dwell on the negative, surrounding themselves with dark energy and bad vibes. Not all women are *playa hataz,* but many have *hata* tendencies (that often stem from their insecurities), which can still trip up any stroll down Closing the Deal Avenue.

Knowing that *playa hatin'* can be a problem, we figured that diagnosing the problem is half the battle. Therefore, we've created the following list of questions to enable you to discover if you are a *playa hata,* have *playa hata* tendencies, or are surrounded by them.

How to Identify a *Playa Hata:* A Mini-Quiz

Note: All *playa hataz* in the quiz below are of the female persuasion.

1. True or False

   When you walk into a bar, the first thing you notice is the other women. Did you answer true? Uh-oh. *Playa hataz* are often guilty of committing this number-one catty-woman faux pas.

2. Be honest! You've cried at your girlfriends' weddings because

   a. it wasn't you who was getting married

   b. the brides were eight years younger than you were, not to mention eighteen pounds lighter

   c. the color of the bridesmaids' dresses (and the gloves) you were asked to wear were always burnt orange

   d. none of the above

   If you answered *d,* you're in the clear. However, if you chose *a, b,* or *c* because you like only weddings at which

---

* For those of you who have been in solitary for the last few years, a *playa hata* is one who is jealous of another because (s)he does not have any game of her/his own. *See also* schadenfreude.

someone objects to the union or dies, you most definitely have issues.

3. *When you are losing a board game, you usually*

   a. quit

   b. don't lose board games. Period.

   c. cheat. After all, it's not as if your two-year-old niece is going to notice or remember it.

   d. none of the above

If you chose *a, b,* or *c,* you're hatin'. If you chose *d* because you never play board games, it doesn't necessarily mean you're not a *hata.* Some *playa hataz* don't play board games because it takes time away from dissing other women.

4. *When you and your coworker have a wee crush on "the new guy," you would never*

   a. lick his cheek in the Monday-morning staff meeting and scream, "Mine! I called him!"

   b. send him demented e-mails from your coworker's account

   c. let the best woman win

   d. place Post-its in your coworker's bag and have her arrested for office-supply theft

This was a trick question. You are in a long-term relationship with a man to whom you want to get hitched, so you are no longer entitled to have crushes on your coworkers. However, if your single coworkers are nice gals, they would chose *c: Playa hataz* don't use the words *woman* and *best* within three sentences of each other.

5. *True or False*

You find it therapeutic to discuss your girlfriends' problems with other girlfriends in public, especially if they are really personal.

True? Then you, girlfriend, are a rude *playa hata.*

If you find yourself hatin', then your man is going to be wondering why you're hatin'. He'll wonder if you're less secure with yourself than you first appeared. He'll be wondering what she's got that you haven't got. We have to assume that if you're in a long-term relationship with a guy, he has plenty of reasons for sticking around. Maybe it's time you looked inward and took stock of all the great things that you're bringing to the relationship. Learning to love other people starts with loving yourself! (Yes, we've watched *Oprah*.)

Being on either end of hatin' can harm *any* deal too. If you find that you're surrounded by *playa hataz*, it's time to go looking for a karma douche somewhere far, far away from your circle of friends. One of our sisters-in-law had a gaggle of "friends" that were clearly not looking out for her best interests. She'd had her suspicions that she was surrounded by people who weren't really rooting for her, but it was confirmed after she lost some weight and not one of them was happy for her. One day she decided she'd had enough of their catty ways. She was single at the time, and it took a lot of strength of character to walk away from her main social circle, but she felt that she'd rather be alone than with this group of *hataz*. We don't think it's a coincidence that within a month she met her future husband.

Negative outside forces can take a toll on any relationship, so be careful not to put yourself in a competitive or *playa hatin'* environment. These forces, however, can be countered with a positive attitude and a refusal to take part in negative campaigning when it comes to winning your boyfriend's vote in the closing-the-deal elections. Just say "no" to competition.

So now that we've covered hatin' and competin', the two no-nos of datin', why don't we discuss some of the yes-yeses.

The Ten MANments

SO WHAT *DO* FAT (WITH AN F) FELICIA AND that ho Shawn have that you haven't got? Maybe they're secure with who they are and haven't been *playa hataȥ* since they were seventeen. Or, maybe it's that they know the **Ten MANments.** Those are the ten personality traits for which men are suckers. Since *Closing the Deal* is as much about creating the foundation for a successful relationship as it is about getting engaged, we think it's important to go over what we believe are the universal qualities that make up successful relationships. This part is not about the hatin', it's about the *lovin'.* So join us as we uncover the magic . . .

First, a little philosophical discussion: Let's say you believe in the concept of soul mates. That means that you're not overwhelmed by the notion that there are mathematically thousands of potential mates for everyone and an exponential amount of possible pairings. It also means that you're the kind of person who is reading this book because you're frustrated that the man you are with, whom you believe to be your soul mate, needs some convincing. The fact that you're not engaged might indicate that your man doesn't entirely subscribe to the theory of soul mates. While you're wondering about the existence of true love, he's calculating the statistical odds on whether an individual, coupled at random from the universal pool of single people, has a decent chance of a happy marriage. So here's the question: If your man isn't so sure that you're his soul mate, how do you convince him that you are? Really, how do you make your man feel comfortable about moving forward when he expresses the possibility of the success of your union as $\Sigma((a^*z)!Sin/3 + \Psi/X(2))$?

Well, we've solved the theorem for you with Ten MANments, which, when tailored to your man, will make him start to believe that he's found his destiny—you. Inspired by the religious code, the Ten MANments are the solid foundation to a civilized coexistence. As this chapter is meant to help you direct your man's attention to where it should be (you), we would be remiss if we didn't cover the things that you *should* be instead of just what you shouldn't.

Whether he's a banker, a car salesman, a lawyer, a cop, a writer, a bus driver, an accountant, or a doctor, there are some fairly universal things that a man looks for in a wife. These are the staples of a relationship, like food, air, and water are the staples of life. Like the original Ten Commandments, it's rarely okay to break them (unless you're willing to deal with the consequences). While the Marriage Motivators cover what will get your boyfriend excited about marriage, the Ten MANments will cover what will get—and keep—your boyfriend excited about you.

1. Self-Respect

We could probably put it more eloquently than William Shakespeare did in *Hamlet*, but we would hate to have to embarrass him in this kind of setting. He wrote, *"This above all: to thine own self be true, and it must follow, as the night the day, thou canst not then be false to any man."* Though he was referring to honesty, the same can be said for love. If you can't love yourself, no man can love you. Self-respect manifests itself in many shapes and forms, whether it's keeping yourself well groomed or meditating to create some inner calm, a woman who appreciates herself is easily discernible from one who does not. Yes, it's part confidence (really believing in yourself takes guts), but it's also about learning to *like* yourself—the opposite of *playa hatin'*.

2. Attention

This just in: men have giant egos. Bar fights and world wars can often be boiled down to those large and fragile egos. If just a few more women would make the effort to soothe our tenuous sense of self by repeatedly telling us how great we are (and getting us to believe it), we would all be one day closer to world peace. It's called many things (doting, mothering, etc.), but a woman who pays attention, who is aware of and anticipates her man's feelings, whether they are physical or emotional, makes a powerful and lasting impression.

As you may have noticed, men aren't exactly the greatest communicators when it comes to expressing their feelings. Men are not going to spell out when they're feeling neglected by saying, "Pay attention to me; I want to feel important," but men love to be reassured, at least every once in a while, that they are the center of your world.

Don't take the attention thing too far, though. Asking him to recount his entire day at work minute by minute isn't what we have in mind. Asking him how his day was and listening to the answer is more like it. Other ways of paying attention include anticipating when he wants to be left alone. Okay, we know this sounds a bit tough to navigate, and it is, but you need to find the balance between the amount of attention he wants and the amount of space he wants and give it to him (he must do the same for you, the point being to make each of you happy). Hopefully you can find a place in your relationship (perhaps you already have?) at which this becomes natural and not a laborious process. Don't overanalyze this (like we have); most of the time the balance is instinctual.

3. Loyalty

We can't think of one example when a spouse shouldn't put their other half first. Though you're not eternally linked yet, your mate had better see the seeds of loyalty early on or he'll be looking to drop his seed elsewhere. We don't mean that if you find out you're dating a serial killer you have to stick around for the trial, but, at a minimum, defend your man's honor when his friend accuses him of cheating at golf. Discretion is also a part of loyalty; don't overly confide in your girlfriends about things that your boyfriend has overly confided in you.

It might sound feudalistic, but your boyfriend's honor should be important to you, even at the expense of your own comfort. A friend of one of us, Steven, was at a black-tie silent auction with his girlfriend, Sara, and about to bid on an item when the auctioneer declared the auction over. Another guy, standing nearby with his date, grabbed the clipboard from Steven and said that it was too late to bid, calling Steven a cheater and creating a bit of a scene. The name caller's date immediately walked away from the incident, but not Sara. Knowing that Steven was many things, including nonconfrontational, but that a cheater was not one of them, not only did Sara take it upon herself to put this guy in his place, but she also spent time telling anyone who would listen what a wonderful person Steven was. When they left the party, Steven thanked Sara for all the nice things she had said. Sara smiled and told Steven that she'd do it again, even though the guy probably had a point about Steven being too late to bid. How's that for loyalty? That was just one of the many things that helped Sara close the deal.

4. Character

Ah, yes. The moral fiber located in one's backbone. You've seen the T-shirts—BEHIND EVERY GREAT MAN IS A GREAT WOMAN—and now you can live it! Character is the sum total of many traits—decency, compassion, and honesty, to name just three. We have yet to come across a man on this earth who is consciously looking to marry beneath him (at least the first time around). Whether you've cheated on your taxes or past boyfriends, men don't want to marry a scandal magnet. Just take a look at Tony Soprano. Even the lowest forms of humanity want to be with a woman who not only can distinguish right from wrong but also chooses correctly. As a general rule, guys don't marry women who are more morally corrupt than they are. (For many men, this may be because there aren't any.) If your past is filled with a few bad decisions, learn from them. If they ever come up, hopefully you can look him straight in the eye and tell him that you learned from past mistakes and that you'll never do (whatever it was) again because the experience was too painful.

5. Sense of Humor

The next time you read the personals, count how many times women say a variant of "Nothing is sexier than a sense of humor." This is another way of saying, "Nothing is sexier than a guy who can make a great situation better and who can stay positive when things take a turn for the worse." It's also a nice way of saying, "No matter how ugly you are, I can still laugh with you and at you." So why shouldn't the reverse be true as well? A woman with a sense of humor is a beautiful thing. Not only can she crack the occasional joke, but she would never roll her eyes at ours.

6. Gentle Nature

Generally, men don't want a woman who's more masculine than they are. We have met quite a few women who have the misconception that most guys want to marry a girl who is one of the guys. Maybe in high school guys *thought* they wanted to marry the tomboy next door, but for the most part femininity is a quality that men crave. While it is true that a woman's "hangability" is an added incentive (see Marriage Motivator 3, "What's a Blow Job Between Friends?"), it should never be at *the expense of* her womanliness. For example, having a wife who can explain the infield fly rule to her husband's buddy from Venezuela is lovely, but not while she's peeing in a urinal standing up. This is not just about acting feminine; it's also about looking and feeling it as well. You should consider your soft skin, gentle touch, soothing voice, and sensuous smell the currency that will help you close the deal.

7. Companionability

Being a good companion is a combination of many things, but this MANment is mostly about being a good friend, listener, activity partner, and caregiver. Finding things that you enjoy doing together will help any relationship (see "Lobby for a Mutual Hobby," page 38). As long as you have found things that you enjoy doing together, the relationship will almost take care of itself, whether the activity is cooking, hiking, sailing, watching TV, or praying (while watching sports on TV). A woman who often looks for new and exciting ways to spend time with her man is a woman seeking marriage for all the right reasons. As you get older, however, the things you enjoy doing together will invariably change, so having companionability also means having flexibility when it comes to exploring activities to do together.

Companions should crave each other's company regardless of what they're doing. They should know when to give comfort and when to give a kick in the pants. A great companion is helpful, trustworthy, selfless, and stable. When thinking about the long term, finding a woman with companionability is like an insurance policy on the marriage. It means when the wheelchair path gets rocky, you'll be right there, bumpin' along next to him.

8. Aura/Karma

We couldn't tell you what exactly these things are, but we do know that when we meet someone with a good aura and positive karma, we like her. Keeping a positive outlook and behaving nobly will serve you well in all aspects of life, not just marriage. Positive auras and good karma are practically irresistible. So if in life you get what you give—give the goodness.

9. Consistency

A lot of what we cover in this book is behavioral, mostly because we know that learning how to control one's words and actions is a lot more doable than learning how to control one's emotions. All three of these things (your words, actions, and emotions), must have a modicum of consistency. Look, we can't give you an aura transplant or an attitude adjustment pill, but we *can* ask you to reflect on your emotional stability (see Chapter 5).

Consistency translates into stability, and that's an important quality to have for the long haul. For example, if you cry during every argument, your tears will lose impact quickly and your man will question how stable you are. We are not suggesting that men don't want spontaneity . . . just keep in mind that what we really want is a consistent "yes" every time we ask if you're cool with us going to a bachelor party followed by a consistent kiss when we return.

10. Effort

Which came first, apathy or divorce? Who cares? We do. We'd venture that apathy is the Biggest Relationship Killer of All Time. It's what comes after the relationship has run its course but before it has ended. Whether you've been fighting a lot lately or things are going great, your relationship should never run on cruise control. It may sometimes feel like this requires a Herculean effort—you might have to do things that are contrary to your stubborn nature—but it's really important that your man doesn't think that you're the type to throw in the towel if things aren't going right. Little efforts, like apologizing first after a stupid argument, are a great way to show that you will always be looking to make things better. He'll appreciate you even more for it, because although he'll know he was just as much at fault as you were, if you appeal to his ego (see MANment 2) he'll be in awe of you even more.

And no, we don't have a double standard here. Your man should reciprocate all of these *in triplicate.* If he doesn't, then you may want to check out Chapter 9, "Cutting Bait."

The great thing about the Ten MANments is that if you obey them faithfully, it will really seem to him that you are the only woman in the world.

Selling It Through

YOU COULD PRETTY MUCH HAVE THIS BOOK memorized and even employ much of the advice, but if you're not selling your virtues, your boyfriend won't be buying them. Any great salesman will tell you that the easiest way to sell something is to truly believe in it ("Never sell an empty box" is a famous salesman's line). Once you put all the childhood traumas, the pretty dramas, the underwhelming self-image, and your *playa hatin'* ways behind you and remind yourself that you have the greenest grass in the neighborhood, everyone—especially your man—will want to play on it.

Great qualities should be flaunted, whether you're marketing products, films, or people, especially in today's world. Not every action has to be "big" or "dramatic," but when your gentle nature or your loyalty shows up in simple or mundane ways, it can often mean so much more. In certain situations, the soft sell can be as effective as the hard one. For example, if he loves your sense of humor, you don't have to do a stand-up routine at dinner; it's enough to just make him laugh once in a while.

So if you're still wondering why Fat Felicia or that ho Shawn closed the deal, then you have failed to realize the most important lesson of all in *Closing the Deal:* Deal closers show the men in their lives that they have exactly what their men want. Every step of the way, these women make their men feel like they're winning gold at the marriageathon.

5 Your Emotional Makeup: How Much to Apply?

IF WE HAD TO SUM UP THIS CHAPTER IN TWO words made of eight letters and an apostrophe, it would look like this: Your 'Tude.

Each and every woman has been blessed with a unique emotional makeup. How much of it you can apply when handling your man certainly depends a lot on his own emotional level. Some men can handle and appreciate your emotional fluctuations, while others recoil or go on the offensive when a tear is shed or a voice is raised. You need to know your man and how much emotion he's up for, and you must also know yourself and your proclivity for high drama. After all, if you're a squishy emotional sponge and you need lots of affection and attention and your man has the emotional range of Sheetrock, he might not be the guy who can fulfill you (or handle you) long term.

There are some general things we can help you understand about the male species when it comes to emotions, and we're happy to provide you with a few tips on how to handle your man and yourself.

Not long ago, we too read the books about how men and women have ventured forth from different planetary bodies, and we concurred then, as most people did, that the differences between men and women go far beyond the physical. The fact is, you gals know how different we are in *practical* terms but often fail to take this into consideration in your day-to-day interactions with your dude.

Planet Man

MOST OF THE MEN WE POLLED CAN GO TO sleep in the middle of a heated argument with their wives or girl-friends and have a peaceful night's rest, while their women lie awake, tossing and turning, aching to wake up their man and explore the argument ad infinitum. Men generally don't let their mood envelop or overpower their interactions as much as women. In our experience, men are somewhat less susceptible to extreme mood swings. In other words, when it comes to moods, men are a bit more *predictable*.

Women we know, on the other hand, often have different responses to similar stimuli at different times. (Yes, this is a blatant generalization and a cliché, but it's also generally true, and many of the women we spoke to readily copped to it.) We know we're treading on thin ice here and don't want to completely lose *our* audience, so let us get to the point: If it's deal closing you want, you're going to need to make your man feel like he's marrying the Michael Jordan of wedlock: steady, in control, and graceful under pressure, despite the many emotional upheavals you may be facing.

Having spoken with men of varying sensibilities, we have concluded that *Closing the Deal*'s worst enemy is the single woman who can be (pick one) irrational, oversensitive, emotionally indulgent, unrealistic, or—how should we say this?—overly controlling. In fact, a woman's actions under pressure are taken into heavy consideration when men are deciding if they're going to leave you or close the deal. Women often set the tone for the relationship, and if you tend to be nasty, argumentative, bitter, or defensive (i.e., *playa hatin'*), you may already be on rocky turf.

Your Monthly Visit from Aunt Flo

WE EXPECT MOST OF OUR HATE MAIL TO dwell on the next section; nevertheless, we need to spend time discussing your monthly hormonal hoedown. We figure if loads of women can dish about how bloated and angry they get, why can't we? Whether or not it's the cause, PMS often takes the blame for the emotional swings known to occur in most women.

Most Men Are Clueless

The truth is, many men are clueless about menstruation, especially if they've never had to buy tampons for their sister (or don't have one). Most men don't know all that much about bodily functions, and certainly can't relate to mood swings each month; thus any mood swing can seem completely and utterly foreign and irrational to your man, leaving your period to take the blame even if it's not that time of the month. Of course, if you are hormonal and raging, it doesn't mean you're not entitled to a release of your emotions. Just keep in mind that when you're deal closing, you need to make an effort to keep your moods in check, so as not to confuse Mr. Right.

Men can be immature about many things, but especially your period. This could be because we don't have anything nearly as dramatic happen to us on a monthly basis and thus have an inability to identify with you. The best thing you can do is let your partner know that you're actually getting your period and are not feeling well. This information will help him understand how you are feeling as opposed to leaving him frustrated and confused as to why he may have to tiptoe around you.

PMS or not, irrational behavior at any time can not only prevent you from closing the deal, but also increase the probability that your man's reaction will be "Who the hell did I get myself involved with?" Regardless of your period, we think it's never too late to rehash the how-tos of self-control.

Whether it's mood swings, postwork 'tude, or anything else, we're here to offer you some self-control tips. How do you handle big issues as a lovely sweet lady would (even if you're bloated and cramping) and still stand your ground on subjects ranging from The Prenup to I Hate His Mother? Here are some basic rules:

1. Think *before* you speak.
2. Think *while* you're speaking.
3. Think about what you *just* said (and consider explaining or apologizing if you think you need to).

Basically, if you know that once a month you're prone to throw a temper tantrum or a phone (regardless of Aunt Flo), it doesn't mean your situation is hopeless. It just means that you're going to have to make more of an effort to keep things together as your clueless guy's eyes glaze over.

It's Still No Excuse

Whatever the wonderful excuse for your high drama, good common sense should always prevail when it comes to your relationship, familial, and work interactions. Everyone appreciates a little "honesty" every once in a while, but sometimes people make the mistake of being too up front regarding delicate issues, especially when they're on edge. While you may find any number of things upsetting, frustrating, or unsettling while you're dating or dealing with parents or relatives (or your wannabe in-laws), your ability to demonstrate grace under pressure (mental, emotional, or physical) will pay off in spades. Of course, remember that if you don't swim, you sink, and no amount of cramping will get you out of it.

Power Women, Powerful Interactions

AS WOMEN CONTINUE TO MAKE HUGE strides in the workforce and in politics, a new generation of men is dealing with women who, in many instances, will be more powerful than they are.

Successful women may face a harder time than their male counterparts. Quite simply, it's not considered odd if men in charge yell at their employees; if they do, powerful men are never referred to as "bitches" and no one comments on the cost, style, or color of any businessman's suit or briefcase (well, *we've* never been asked). As two men who are part of this first generation of men to work for successful women and have female mentors, we have been raised "gender blind" and have never wondered "who's the boss" or had any problems with the "new" female roles. So for all of you women out there who are making more money than your man, who can pack a punch with the best of them, you get kudos from us.

However, all Americans are not gender neutral. And your future father- or mother-in-law may not feel the same way as you and your man about your career. But luckily you're not marrying them; it's their son you want. All the same, as you get to know them, if they do take issue with your having a career, there are ways to fix the situation—or make it worse. To fix it, you should obviously watch your 'tude.

When women are powerful at the office, like their male counterparts, they sometimes bring the power home, which can affect the level and temperature of many conversations. The stress of a day at work—in addition to family issues—could create or underscore an emotional situation. Of course this goes for both sexes, but bringing home and displacing your anger or stress is something of which you need to be aware and careful when you're trying to close the deal. Whether you're the boss or on your way there, don't bring her home for dinner, especially if she's in a bad mood.

Let's look at a friend of ours who applied a little too much power play and almost suffered from a nonmerger.

Carrie and Dimitri

CARRIE IS A SUCCESSFUL investment banker in Boston. She thrives on the energy, being part of the boys' club, and the power she wields in a very cutthroat business. When she's not at the office Carrie can be found closing deals at a Red Sox game or the golf course. We'd describe her as cool and calculating. Two years ago she married Dimitri, a very good-looking insurance broker, who is a bit more low-key. He's no pushover, mind you—he's very opinionated and has a strong sense of right and wrong. People are naturally drawn to Dimitri, as he has traveled the world and has extensive knowledge on a variety of subjects. As a couple, they are equally balanced in that they both feel they got a deal: He's a sexy, good guy and she's principled, attractive, and—best of all—generates much more coin.

Carrie has been known to raise her voice a few decibels in the course of making a business deal. While the other bankers occasionally do the same, it's the norm with Carrie. She's prone to outbursts when she doesn't get her way, and she's even admitted that when she's bloated she can be as scary as a Stephen King novel. When people pass by her office, they listen in awe as she berates colleagues or whomever else is on the other end of the phone. As she brings in a lot of money for her bank, most of the senior executives (not all of whom are men, by the way) look the other way, so no one is really sure whether Carrie was ever made aware that her behavior causes a good deal of discomfort and anxiety among her peers and subordinates.

But Carrie is no fool: As tough a businesswoman as she is, when it comes to her bosses and her clients, she's all charm and grace. And more important, she is able to leave the stress at work.

At home and around her friends and family, she is the extraordinarily engaging, likeable, and humorous woman Dimitri fell in love with.

Carrie loves Dimitri and always gives him the royal treatment; yet when they were first engaged she had to work hard not to overreact to her new, somewhat demanding in-laws-to-be. In fact, Carrie once pushed Dimitri so hard on a family issue that they got into a huge fight and almost broke up. Carrie wanted to throw Thanksgiving, which traditionally was always done by her future sister-in-law. When it became clear to Carrie that Thanksgiving dinner wasn't going to be hers, Carrie switched into work mode to get what she wanted—and let loose in front of Dimitri's mother, raising her voice, making accusations, and creating a whole other set of problems. Dimitri had never seen this other side of his intended and was embarrassed at what he thought was inappropriate behavior. He thought Carrie had overreacted, especially since they weren't even married yet. Dimitri was concerned for weeks, wondering if she was the right girl, especially after his mother expressed her own concern. While Dimitri often took Carrie's side on issues, he let her know that he would not tolerate her recent behavior in front of his mother and that he would hold her accountable if she didn't keep her "office skills" in check.

Carrie was upset by Dimitri's change in behavior toward her, and was so embarrassed that she had gone so haywire, that she made a mental note *never* to engage Dimitri or his mother and other in-laws in an antagonistic way again, or she knew it would be a deal breaker. She realized that Dimitri had a point. Emotional tirades and temper tantrums were not the way to get what she wanted in their relationship. She decided to make a change, and in order to make the transition easier she decided to think of her future mother-in-law as she would a business client. By turning on all the charm, grace, and "client service" she used every day in her professional life, she was soon able to set a new standard for her relationship with her in-laws.

Whether we agree with Carrie's tactics or not—we don't believe in shutting oneself down, just watching your mouth—her new behavior didn't change once she got married. She realized she loved Dimitri enough to smile and nod when her mother-in-law was around. Carrie will never be a pushover, however; she's just learned to take deep breaths before she speaks. She's also made huge efforts to bond with her in-laws and brings their extended families together by planning family trips, buying thoughtful presents, and helping out when she can. And everyone is happy.

NOW WHILE THIS EXAMPLE may seem extreme, there's an important lesson here: Even the most powerful, expressive women out there can make a concerted effort to decide how they want their relationship to turn out and, if need be, check their 'tude at the door.

What we learned: You might not love all your clients, business associates, or customers, but they still pay the bills, so you manage to be nice to them. Why not apply this theory to your in-laws (or anyone else, for that matter)? After all, giving your new mom or dad "client service" is a lot easier than fighting them every step on the way to the altar.

Getting to Know You and Other Relationship Killers

THERE ARE A HANDFUL OF MATTERS COUPLES fight over while in the dating phase, and a whole new set arises during the engagement. In both cases, we believe they can all be resolved for the long term if couples establish ground rules early on. Here's some advice on how you might address and resolve some possible dating deal breakers. You may not have encountered these yet, but, either way, it's always good to be prepared. Keep in mind that the advice below is tailored to female readers; while men always have half the responsibility on these issues, this book is about *your* half of the transaction.

Dating Deal Breakers
BACHELOR HABITS

How long your man has been single will dictate a lot of things, including how much he's willing to adapt to your behavioral requests. From personal hygiene to apartment cleanliness, his habits may be so ingrained that for the life of him he can't understand why you make a big deal when he drinks straight from the orange juice carton or neglects to empty the dishwasher.

Assuming you're in serious date/sleepover mode and you've registered your simple complaints with him (e.g., picking up his socks from the floor, putting the toilet seat down, etc.) more than once and things aren't changing, what's next? It's not as if you can complain to his supervisor. The good news is that we believe you *can* teach an old bachelor new tricks. It's just that getting your man to change his habits takes time, effort, and plenty of positive reinforcement. What it boils down to is this: Screaming and nagging will not work. If you want results, you're going to have to be smart about it. Nice, too. *Nag* is almost a four-letter word.

We find that when it comes to sensitive subjects like toilet seat etiquette and other personal hygiene issues, men appreciate a good sense of humor, so go down the smile aisle. Why not get creative when trying to retrain your man? One smart and funny gal we know was so fed up that she glued a spring contraption to the toilet seat so it would automatically go down. Another clever woman we know put the dirty dishes her man left in the sink in his briefcase before he left for work. The important thing here is that these women criticized with a sense of humor—not at their man's expense, and *not* out of anger. And it will work for you just the same.

After all, a lot of guys already have one mom who's been nagging them for years, and they're probably not looking for a replacement.

THE SMALL STUFF

The best advice we give our soon-to-be-married friends is to pick your battles. Do you live for sushi while he gets seasick looking at fish tanks? Do you both prefer the aisle seat to the window? Do you like to go skiing on your winter vacations while he likes to bake in the sun? Apparently, even with all of this little stuff, you still like him enough to want to marry him.

How do you solve some of these issues? Just remember to ask yourself what you really *are* bothered about. If he's chivalrous, he'll give you the aisle seat, and if you're reasonable, you'll do sushi with your girlfriends and save him from the mercury poisoning. And if you love each other you'll do a winter *and* a sun vacation each year, if you can afford it (or just switch off). When one party is winning all the arguments, it won't translate into a winning relationship. It *never hurts* to throw up the white flag or to compromise once in a while. You might be surprised at how a little concession or two makes a very big statement about how much you love him. (Of course, you shouldn't be doing all the giving all the time . . . but for these situations, let's pretend you owe him one.)

If your man shows up at a party wearing the same shirt as another guy, odds are they'll become friends for life. In other words, real men aren't genetically wired to sweat the small stuff, so don't make them start. Most men we know are happy to give in to the small stuff if they feel that you can give in on something that's small to them but big to you. (Check out the next point and you'll know what we mean.) So think things through, especially before you speak, and compromise often. We don't want you to regret anything.

BUDDIES, BACHELOR PARTIES,
AND BOYS' NIGHTS OUT

Spending free time together should be a priority for both of you, but if you give him a hard time about seeing his buddies or attending a bachelor party, you will no doubt be engaging in one of the oldest relationship battles around. Interestingly, most men we know think that hanging out with their best buddies, like at a bachelor party, should be no big deal; however, this is a classic example of what could be no big deal for him but a very big deal for you.

Hopefully, once you're dating seriously, spending time together won't be an issue in your relationship. Of course, the right amount of time allocation doesn't mean Every Last Minute. Too much of anything can be unhealthy.

If you have a problem with your boyfriend's spending too much time (or any time) with his friends, then you have to ask yourself *why*. If it's because you don't trust him when he's with them and you feel that they are a bad influence on him, then keeping him away from his friends isn't going to solve your underlying trust issues. We suggest that you work hard at this. Trust is a huge element in any relationship, and your trying to control his time away from you is the least healthy solution we can think of.

On the other hand, if the problem with your future fiancé is that he works hundred-hour weeks and *then* chooses to go golfing or spend sizable chunks of his only free time with his friends, then you, girlfriend, have a right to feel slighted or at *least* take it as a sign. Give your man the freedom to spend time with his buddies, but let him know that if he doesn't watch it, too much time away from you may mean he'll be on his own time, full time, in a short time.

Lastly, when it comes to bachelor parties, most women we know get a nervous twitch at the sound of "Las Vegas." Visions of bodacious blondes doing lap dances or other more salacious acts can certainly be unnerving in the abstract. Our POV is that you're marrying either someone who will be faithful or someone who won't. If you have a trusting, respectful relationship, a weekend with the boys won't get a guy who's on the straight and narrow to stray. However, if you can't trust him in Vegas (or any strip club), chances are you can't trust him at the office either.

EX MARKS THE SPOT

Maintaining friendships with exes is a complicated issue. How do you find a solution that works for you and your man without either of you overreacting? This is such a complicated issue, it's the one area where our opinions differ. Therefore, we'll share both with you.

DANIEL SAYS: If it bothers your boyfriend (and you want to marry him), then it should bother you too. It's up to both of you to decide whether maintaining a relationship with an ex is cool. A healthy relationship requires *two* mentally stable participants, and if your man is the jealous type, then all the reassuring conversations in the world won't make him any calmer that your ex is still somewhere in the picture (even if he *is* in the background). If your man can't come to terms with the role that your ex plays in your life, then the ex needs to go. And if that means missing some parties or putting some effort into making your current flame/future fiancé feel comfortable, that's just what you should do.

That's not to say that you shouldn't try to make it work. However, if there's no peaceful solution, then you need to put the *over* in "ex-lover." Sad to say, it doesn't matter that your ex was there for you when your poodle died or that you have great memories from college that you still want to hold on to. You're not closing the deal with him. Of course, if there is still some question as to how you feel about your ex, you need to reevaluate your current relationship. If you can't live without him, then do it at your own peril. Just know that whatever you do, *do not* do it behind your future fiancé's back.

RICHARD SAYS: I do agree with Daniel that if it bothers your boyfriend it should bother you and vice versa. However, I live more in the gray than Daniel on this issue. As many couples nowadays get married later in life, there are many instances in which ex-lovers have evolved into great friends. So from personal experiences (or those of my good friends who've enlightened me), I have three simple rules that will make your life much easier.

Rule 1: If an ex-boyfriend is now your friend, don't expect your boyfriend/fiancé to be friends with him. You can have a friendship on your own time; just keep it to lunches and *be sure* to tell your man about it!

Rule 2: If ten years go by and you can't remember the sex, it's a pretty good indication that this person is really a friend. However, having one or, at most, two such friends is acceptable. More than four and it's a basketball team.

Rule 3: This is an exception, not a rule. *Don't* bring him up (as a subject) in mixed company. It's never comfortable for your current flame/wannabe future fiancé to hear about all your previous lovers and how wonderful they are. Keep it to a minimum.

No matter how big or small the issue is, keeping your relationship sane and smooth is the best tool to keep things going well. We'll talk more about your engagement period a bit later, but for now, just remember: If you and your lover are making strides in your relationship, then it's always wise to try to keep the momentum going. Nagging and fighting, no matter the subject, are always relationship busters.

You May Need to Check into AA . . .
Take Our Attitude Aptitude Quiz

SO WHAT HAPPENS IF YOU'VE BEEN DATING for a year and there are still a few outstanding issues that need to be resolved? Suddenly, after reading this section, you're not sure whether you have attitude issues or your behavior is entirely justified—you've been fighting a bit, but you don't know if it's healthy or unhealthy conflict. Maybe a few more things will be clarified for you when you look at a few popular scenarios and see how our sample girlfriend Sally and her boyfriend Billy deal with them.

1. Sally comes home to see Billy's socks on the floor. Sally can't count how many times she told Billy to pick up his socks. They've been dating for two years, and it isn't looking as though Billy's getting any better at sock detail. What should Sally do?
   a. Pick up the socks and put them in the hamper and say nothing.
   b. Put the socks under Billy's pillow and say nothing.
   c. Scream and yell because screaming and yelling works if done over extended periods of time.
   d. Ignite the socks using butane and firebomb the sleeping Billy while screaming, "Incoming, soldier!"
   We recommend *b*. *A* says, "I'm a pushover"; *b*, on the other hand, says, "You may not think you have to change, but I do." Plus, something like this will still show your sense of humor. It takes the edge off this very old conversation while still saying, "I'm serious" in only a minimally threatening way. While *c* and *d* may be a bit overboard, if you're screaming over socks, you might as well pack it in now before you start getting angry about heavier objects.

2. Billy gets a call from his ex-girlfriend, Princess, with whom he broke up three years before. Apparently her father, King Charles of Spaniel, has disinherited her because she failed to bring home her second consecutive Nobel Prize in literature and is falling back on her modeling career while she finishes her joint MBA/JD degree at Harvard. Billy asks Sally if she would mind if he goes to console her for an hour in her penthouse suite at the Four Seasons. What should Sally say?

   a. "Sure, Billy. Don't forget condoms." (Sweetly)
   b. "I don't really feel comfortable with this arrangement. Can she come here?" (Calm but serious)
   c. "Are you *expletive* crazy?" (Most serious)
   d. "The Princess needs to find someone else to call. It's been three years since you two dated." (Firm but serious)

   Both *b* and *d* work. It really all depends on what Sally is comfortable with. *D* is more than appropriate if Sally is even the slightest bit uncomfortable with Princess's role in their lives. Like most men, Billy will probably press Sally on this issue. It doesn't matter if Billy says that he'd let Sally go if the situation were reversed. If Sally doesn't like the situation, then there is no reason that Billy needs to go to that hotel room. If Sally is in a more generous mood, they can invite Princess over for tea and crumpets. And if Sally doesn't know what a crumpet is, Billy should tell Princess to pick some up on her way over. End of story.

3. Billy's best friend, Bob, is getting married in a few weeks, and Bob wants Billy, his best man, to plan a bachelor party in Las Vegas. Billy is up to the task, but Sally wants to set some ground rules first. What should Sally's overriding sentiment be for Billy's trip?

a. "You can go, depending on what your definition of 'is' is." (Pacing)

b. "Call me the moment you are about to cheat on me." (Tears)

c. "I trust you. Have fun but be respectful." (Slap on the back)

d. "Billy, I think you know better than to ask me for permission. Of course, you *can't* go." (Pointing the finger)

Most of you would guess the correct answer is *c*. Good. If you can't see yourself uttering those trusting words, then get to work fixing that trust problem. The same thing that was true for your parents holds true for you: When your parents left you alone in the house for a weekend when you were in high school and said that they trusted you, it echoed in your head the whole time you were thinking about throwing the party of the century but didn't. We have faith in our brethren and virtually guarantee that when he's gambling and going to strip clubs, he will have his fun but will still maintain the sanctity of your bond.

4. Billy occasionally blurts out inappropriate things at all sorts of social occasions. As the comments are generally harmless, Sally considers this part of Billy's charm and takes it in stride. Tonight, in front of Sally's boss, Billy talks about his great experience with an underage prostitute in Thailand. Sally should

a. laugh and blame Billy's medication.

b. smile, wait until she is alone with Billy, and firmly reprimand him in private.

c. slap him across the face and storm off.

d. poke him in the ribs and try to top the story with the one about her, the chess team, and the shoe horn.

C sure would be nice, huh? But since Sally's a lady, she will go with *b*. Whatever Sally decides, however, she should do it in private. Don't hesitate to bring up what he said that you felt was inappropriate. Discussing bad behavior immediately following is a great policy for limiting resentment and resolving the matter in question.

5. Billy and Sally are celebrating the second anniversary of their first date. They have a very active sex life, and so after a few bottles of Merlot, back at Billy's apartment Billy suggests they try something new. Sally offers a 1978 Zinfandel, but Billy says that he meant that he wants her to dress up as a schoolgirl and stay after class for some private lessons. Sally should

   a. speed-dial her mom on the cell and scream, "You were right—Billy's a pervert!"

   b. deadpan, "Sure, Professor, just like old times."

   c. ask, "Where do you keep your formal Scottish kilt, Billy?"

   d. exclaim, while throwing a dishtowel at him, "Grow up, Billy. Your choices are missionary or solitary."

   Save for any religious reasons, the correct answer here is *c*. All men keep an extra kilt around for just this kind of special occasion.

6. Billy has flatulence problems. He can practically fart the alphabet, and Sally justifiably has a problem with that. Recently, Billy has been performing a few too many Dutch ovens (wherein he passes gas in bed and then pulls the sheets over Sally and him to keep the scent trapped). Sally, who never found this funny to begin with (lighten up, Sally), is at her wit's end, because it's a little too reminiscent of her brother and her high school boyfriend, Brutus. The next time Billy tries this, Sally should

a. scream and yell until Billy gets the point.

b. laugh along with Billy and then call the Dutch Oven Hotline.

c. boil Billy's pet rabbit.

d. just shut up and enjoy the special times they share.

If you guessed *a*, then you're getting good at this. While you know that we never advocate screaming, in this instance you can scream all you want. There are times when Billy needs to be put in line, and this is one of them. Dutch ovens are for Hansel and Gretel, not mature relationships. Women shouldn't be treated like one of the boys! (Though it can be funny, once.)

7. Sally, a brunette, and Billy are enjoying a nice brunch at an outdoor café with their friends Kelly and Dave. Mid-conversation, Billy's attention is diverted to a young, slim blond woman in a short skirt. Sally isn't sure that Dave and Kelly have noticed the indiscretion, but she is nevertheless embarrassed. Afterward, she confronts Billy by saying:

a. "Don't give me the BS about how you thought you knew her from high school. You were home-schooled."

b. "You shouldn't want to check out other women, especially in front of my friends. That's disrespectful and embarrassing to me."

c. "I would care if she weren't so fat."

d. "No matter how many girls you check out in front of other people, everyone will still think you're gay."

Any one of these should do the trick, as long as she says it calmly and, of course, in private.

8. Sally and Billy arrive late to Billy's parents' for Christmas dinner. Billy's mom does not appreciate tardiness, but that isn't the whole problem. In the middle of dessert,

Billy, bored with the conversation, decides to liven things up by announcing that Sally doesn't believe in Jesus and thinks the Christmas season is hypocritical. Billy's mom then asks Sally where she plans on spending eternity. Sally, a bit shocked that Billy would say these things (and trying to retain her composure), responds:

a. "Not with you, obviously." (Sarcastically)

b. "Do you really believe all that?" (Confrontationally)

c. "Well, now that I'm with Billy, I'm open to listening to what other people have to say on the issue."

d. "That's absolutely none of your damn business, Mrs. Jones." (Angrily)

C would mean Sally took the high road. If Sally chooses *a*, *b*, or *d*, we hope to have ringside seats for that matchup.

While we don't expect you to take this quiz too seriously, we did want to illustrate that there's always a high road and low road in every conversation or point of tension. How you choose to handle things ranging from small annoyances to larger issues will define your character to those around you.

How Much Emotion Do You Apply?

HOPEFULLY NOT TOO MUCH OF THE ADVICE in this chapter runs contrary to the kind of person you already are (or want to be). Take the time to examine the way you approach differences and conflict in your relationship and adjust them accordingly. Your positive overall demeanor and approach to everyday issues will give your man a sense of how wonderful things will be in the long run. Look at your emotional life as one of the crossroads on the road map to closing the deal. It's your choice whether you want to take the bumpy route or the smooth one.

While some men might understand women who cry at the drop of a hat, others may be genuinely stoic and have a hard time when women show too much emotion, anger, or tears. Some men we spoke to have said that they have absolutely no idea *what* to do when their women express even a bit more emotion than usual. We're not saying you should hide, repress, or camouflage your emotions; we are saying that you should be aware of how you apply your emotional makeup. When you're deal closing, it's not a bad idea to take a look in the mirror once in a while to check out whether you're laying it on too thick or covering up just right.

6 The Scheherazade Factor

Sche·her·a·zade. (shə-ˌher-ə-ˈzäd) *n.* A skilled woman storyteller.

You may be familiar with the story of Scheherazade, the heroine of a popular folktale set in the Middle East. If not, the gist of the story is that every night a sultan demands a new woman, whom he has strangled at daybreak. Scheherazade, an exotic young woman, is brought before the sultan and once there tells him a complex and fascinating tale. She amuses the sultan with her saga and, in order to keep him captivated, suddenly excuses herself and promises to return the following evening. The young sultan hungers not only for the beautiful maiden but also for the conclusion of the intricately woven fable. After she returns, he realizes he cannot live without his nightly entertainment, both mentally and physically, and they live happily ever after.

While the Scheherazade story exists in various incarnations, the idea that remains constant is that creating mystery in a relationship can be intensely intoxicating for a man. We call it the **Scheherazade Factor,** and we're going to lay out for you how to successfully weave a captivating web. The Scheherazade Factor is an artful tactic to closing the deal and is something that will serve your marriage equally well.

Although he did not realize it at the time, Richard's first date with his future wife involved this exact complex. While Richard can be a highly energetic and versatile conversationalist (just ask him yourself), he had found dating dull and onerous because the burden would often fall on him to keep the conversation going, to essentially entertain the woman at hand. Richard often felt that he had to be "on" for clients, so being "on" for a date just added yet another pressure to his already stressful life.

On Richard's first dinner date with his wife, Dana, he had been charmed by her loquacious and outgoing manner. For once *his date* was doing most of the talking. Richard was elated with this unusual development, and unlike on most of his previous dates, he found himself relaxed and well entertained, the conversation flowing back and forth. Suddenly, mid-story, Dana abruptly looked at her watch and exclaimed, "I didn't realize how late it is, and I have to be up early in the morning. Why don't I finish the story another time?" Richard was so engrossed, he made a second date to find out what happened, much faster than he had with any other woman. Little did he realize that he was the sub-conscious and willing victim of the Scheherazade Factor. While Dana's Scheherazade instinct was innate and she continued to keep certain things mysterious, she understood the value of leaving her date wanting more.

The moral of the above story is not that you need to be the life of the party, the center of attention, or even a great story-teller. The message that we want you to take with you is that leaving your man wanting more is incredibly seductive, mysterious, and sexy. Often the best part of a date can be what is *not* said—*that* is the point of the story. The air of mystery never loses its potency either, whether you're on a first date or well into your courtship.

Many women think that the first date is an opportunity to lay down rules or divulge intimate and personal information, thinking that in doing so they are appearing open and honest. Whatever the reason, whether it's the advent of reality TV shows like *Joe Millionaire* and *Blind Date*, the cultural shift to more informal dating or some other factor, many people are left with the false impression that first-date protocol includes questions such as, "Tell me about your previous relationships" or "What kind of women are you attracted to?" These are some most unfortunate icebreakers. Not only do these questions sound stock, but they appear somewhat transactional; more akin to hiring the perfect bachelor party stripper than a romantic first date.

Let's take our friend Scheherazade. Do you think she'd ask the sultan point-blank, "So, what are you looking for?" It's okay to want to know the answer to this question, but it's not okay to ask it straight out. If you're not even sure you like the guy (and how can you be sure if you just met him?), why would you care what he's looking for? To some men this line of questioning sounds desperate and insecure, as if you're willing to mold yourself into what he's looking for. Just remind yourself that if the initial dates go well, you'll find out what he likes soon enough.

Right out of the gate, Scheherazade wouldn't talk about her previous relationships or spill the beans on subjects like her abortions, bisexual experiences, or family problems. She would be too consumed with appearing absolutely enigmatic. And unlike the women we see on reality dating shows (we're addicted), she would never jump into a hot tub on the first date with her Prince Charming, even if she fell in love with him on the spot.

Modern-day fairy tales are a lot less misogynistic—women no longer have to tell great stories to save their lives. But a modern-day Scheherazade *can* use her skills to close deals. Read and learn . . .

The Modern-Day Scheherazade: Jennifer

LARRY IS A DIVORCED MULTIMILLIONAIRE in his mid-sixties. Larry has a contagious and boisterous laugh and is a magnet for lighthearted and adventurous people. He's fit and tan and still has some of his hair (although much of it is on his back). He's not retired, but he certainly has more time on his hands now that his children have graduated from college and settled. Needless to say, Larry is quite a commodity, and women have been expressing plenty of interest in him. Said one woman who knows him, "He's adorable, not gay, breathing, and worth over $20 million. Therefore, he may be the sexiest man in America." While she obviously doesn't read *People* magazine, the point is, there's no question that Larry is in demand.

Larry has gone out with socialites, models, and actresses, but he's finally become serious with Jennifer, a forty-seven-year-old divorced real estate agent. Jennifer had been single for more than two years and was hoping to find a husband with whom to travel and enjoy life—someone to grow old with. Jennifer would be the first to say about herself that she is neither a great beauty nor a great intellectual. She's neither rich nor poor, and in many ways she's quite ordinary. So why is it that out of all the women Larry could have chosen, he's chosen Jennifer? To quote Larry, "She makes me feel like I'm the only person in the room."

Jennifer has a great talent many women don't possess. While she's discreet, attentive, funny, and charming, she's most of all a great *listener*. She instinctively avoids looking over Larry's shoulder (or anyone's shoulder, for that matter) when she's engaging him in conversation. She didn't bog Larry down with her problems or issues (initially, anyway). She's seductive without being slutty and mysterious without being aloof. She has the most unusual ability to make whomever she's talking to feel as if he's not only the only person in the room, but in the world.

Strangely enough, Jennifer was late for their first date and apologetically walked up to the bar at the restaurant. She didn't offer any excuse, just said she was sorry that she arrived twenty minutes late. Then Jennifer said, "Sue told me great things about you, but she didn't tell me you had such beautiful blue eyes. Are they from your mother or dad?" For the entire date she said nothing about her ex-boyfriends or the first time she tried marijuana.

At the end of the evening, Jennifer told Larry a genuinely funny story about one of her first jobs. Larry asked her if she had any other funny stories and Jennifer said she had plenty, but that's when she looked at her watch and said, "I have such a long drive ahead of me. Do you mind, Larry, if we continue our evening over the weekend or at my house for dinner?" Jennifer had an instinct for when to keep them wanting more, and Larry was hooked. Scheherazade had struck again! Months later, Larry and Jennifer are still very seriously dating, and Jennifer continues to keep things furtively sexy as all great Scheherazades do. She's still surprising Larry with great stories, dinner parties, new interests, and adventurous friends. She also continues to be his best audience.

When most guys look to close the deal, they hope to have to do it only once. Modern-day Scheherazades know that keeping conversations electrifying *and* being a captivated listener will keep their man sufficiently mesmerized and satiated.

She Sells Scheherazade by the Seashore

WANT TO TRANSFORM YOURSELF INTO A Scheherazade in fifteen minutes or less? It's not that difficult to change your ways. Much of what a good Scheherazade does is subtle—it's often what she *doesn't* do that is most captivating. Because it's all so understated, selling your inner Scheherazade is a lot easier than you think. These pointers should start you on your way:

1. *Find something specific to admire.* Nobody knew this better than President Clinton. We know two women who met him at separate times, and he complimented both of them on their earrings. Very disarming.

2. *Less is more.* It applies here just as it applies to putting on makeup. Scheherazade doesn't tell you she's great; she lets you discover it for yourself.

3. *You're always at the fun table.* All Scheherazades have the confidence to know that no matter where they are, to whom they're talking, or what they're doing, they're always having more fun than anyone and never looking over anyone's shoulder to see if someone is having a better time than they are.

4. *Don't get distracted.* As we've said before, cell phones and other interruptions when you're spending alone time with your man are disrespectful. Scheherazade always put her cell phone on vibrate before she met with the sultan, and so should you.

5. *Know the score.* It's important to be aware of everything around you, especially your boyfriend's mood. Gauge every situation differently. Sometimes just staring lovingly into his eyes and enjoying a quiet moment together is the smoothest Scheherazade move of all.

The Yapper Syndromes

THESE DAYS MANY WOMEN ARE EASILY identified as being victims of **Yapper Syndromes.** A Yapper Syndrome is a fairly recently spawned and culturally accepted but misguided behavioral affliction wherein the Yapper believes everything in a relationship must be up front and visible to all. The Yapper is the opposite of the Scheherazade. She can't wait to tell you all of her secrets and air her dirty laundry. The Yapper can't help herself when it comes to revealing everything about all aspects of her life. She finds her behavior charming, funny, endearing, and/or honest. However, for the most part, revealing too little is ultrasexy, and revealing too much is anything but.

Don't know if you suffer from a case of Yapperitis? It's always good to recognize the problems you may have that can wreck your chances of closing the deal. Let's illustrate a few Yapper Syndromes and hope that we can save a few more souls before we have to declare an epidemic.

Yapper Syndrome 1: "She Can't Keep It to Ho'self"

Renée and Craig have been dating seriously for over a year. While there's not a lot to suggest that they have a terrible relationship, there's not a lot to suggest that they have a great one either. It appears that timing had more to do with their pairing up than true love. They do have a lot in common; both are in their early thirties and each has had an unsuccessful marriage. Both are attractive, successful, and bright, come from nice families, are tired of dating, and want kids.

While Renée and Craig seem on the verge of closing the deal, it appears that Renée has one habit she can't seem to get under control. (Craig is far from perfect, but his issues don't require examination here.) Renée constantly yaps about her personal finances (and previous relationships) to anyone who will listen. Renée talks freely about money—how much she spends at Barneys, how much her new apartment renovation will cost, and how much her previous boyfriends spent on her. Any time Renée does this in public, Craig squirms in his chair, especially when he notices how uncomfortable it can make other people. He finds this behavior affronting on many accounts. Not that Craig is intensely private or hides his success by driving a Pinto, but he believes that Renée's financial affairs (and former affairs) are not for public consumption and are a turnoff to their friends.

Craig has made Renée aware of his feelings more than once, but Renée feels that her openness is what makes people appreciate her no-secrets approach to socializing and making friends. Renée justifies her behavior by saying that she is an "open book" and that's why she's so popular. Craig feels that's just one more reason that she doesn't need to point out her money matters.

The Antidote Renée and Craig and couples like them are headed for crash courses in resentment—from each other and their friends. Unless Renée can accept that her behavior makes other people feel uncomfortable, things aren't going to improve. Perhaps Renée's feelings stem from her insecurity and her way of compensating is to let the world know how successful and sexy she now is and hope they will respect her for it. However, her acquaintances are often embarrassed by her behavior.

For us, the answer is obvious: Don't advertise your personal business. Whether it's former boyfriends, former shopping sprees, or former venereal diseases, keep it to yo'self.

Yapper Syndrome 2: "Let Me Tell You"

Evelyn is a forty-something music video producer from Los Angeles. She's been engaged twice but hasn't been able to close the deal (a copy of the book is on its way, Evelyn). Evelyn always blames the failure of her relationships on her exes, but having socialized with her, we figured out almost immediately that she has a very big issue of her own. (The men she dates may have had other reasons for breaking up with her too, but we'll go with our gut instinct here.)

There was a telltale sign of Yapper Syndrome 2 every time Evelyn began a conversation. It usually started with the phrase "Let me tell you." Once we witnessed a conversation centered on travel, with a couple relaying the details of their recent honeymoon in Prague and how romantic it was. Evelyn countered with, "Well, let me tell you, Prague is fine, but Madrid is where it's *really* happening." Evelyn then supplied countless anecdotes including quotes from travel magazine articles and stories about her friends' experiences there. At the end of the conversation, it became apparent that Evelyn had never even been to Madrid.

Another time, in a conversation about personal grooming techniques (don't ask how we got on that topic), Evelyn quickly dismissed the advice from one of the participants (who just happened to be a world-renowned stylist) and said, "Let me tell you, from personal experience, women prefer shaving to waxing. Not only is it the cheaper and easier way to go, but you don't have to hike across town to some sadomasochistic woman who probably doesn't even sterilize her tools. I can't understand why anyone wouldn't shave. It just shows you how over the top some people can be about grooming. Like I need a male stylist to tell me how to remove hair from my legs." Charming.

If, in any situation, her boyfriend-of-the-moment offered up his own opinion, Evelyn would always be the first one to contradict him. We've seen firsthand the glazed, sullen looks of a few of the potential husbands Evelyn has squashed like a cigarette with her litany of *let me tell yous* and *you don't knows*. It's disheartening.

Many men love the idea of being with an educated woman with well-formed opinions. We each married one. That's not what this Yapper Syndrome is about. (We swear, honey!) "Let me tell you" is not a simple phrase followed by an offering of an opinion; it's a *way of life*. It's an attitude of one-upmanship that manifests itself in an overly aggressive, preaching, and assumptive manner that puts off men and women alike.

Since it is a lifestyle, it shouldn't be surprising that these types often seek the comfort of their own kind. Wherever she goes, Evelyn seeks out other "Let Me Tell You" types. Sadly, these often attractive and smart women—who can't seem to understand why the men all make a neat escape a few weeks into the relationship—are often grouped together in local bars near you. Like a leper to a leper colony, like a harem of *playa hataz*, they find deep comfort in the company of their own because nobody else can tolerate them.

The Antidote "Let Me Tell You" is one of the hardest syndromes to break, since know-it-alls, like all true-blue narcissists, seem to think that they know it all. Hell, when one of the authors tried delicately to bring up to Evelyn an example of another well-known "Let Me Tell You" Yapper (in the hope that she would pick up what one of us was putting down), Evelyn quickly said, "I know the type all too well. Isn't it awful? It's like they don't even recognize that they're doing it." Right.

Why do people become "Let Me Tell You" Yappers? It could be anything from childhood traumas to self-esteem issues. We're not the experts on the whys, but the *why* doesn't really matter. The important thing is recognizing you have it and then doing something about it.

When it comes to deal closing, women who can't tell the difference between interesting banter and incessant barking are closing doors instead of deals. If people keep telling you things like "You're preaching to the converted" or you find yourself trying to top other people's stories, you need to take a good hard look in the mirror. Good conversation isn't about shoving your knowledge, information, and opinions down other people's throats (unless HarperCollins is paying you to do it). A *conversation* is not a diatribe or a monologue. It is, at minimum, a *dialogue*.

Yapper Syndrome 3: "Poor Me"

Penny is a physical trainer from the Midwest. She has a killer body and isn't deficient in the face department either. Because of her attributes and initial approachability, she never lacks for men. Somehow, however, she's been unable to close the deal with any of them.

For some reason, after a few months of getting to know her, men virtually flee. It's not as if Penny isn't sweet, caring, or thoughtful. She is all of those things, not to mention incredibly sincere and reliable. So what's wrong with this picture? Unfortunately for Penny, she's more than a *bit* of a downer.

At first glance, anybody would agree that Penny's life is actually quite fulfilled. She keeps herself busy with activities and remains close with a fun circle of girlfriends. But to Penny, it's a half-empty glass. Relationships never seem to pan out for Penny, and the attention she receives is usually from people feeling sorry for her. If we applied the old expression "You can either be envied or pitied" to Penny, she has obviously chosen the latter, whether she knows it or not.

Though this behavior doesn't cause many problems with her girlfriends and certain men, Penny is a solid example of the third Yapper Syndrome: "Poor Me." Penny just doesn't seem to know how to control her emotions.

While men understand a certain level of insecurity and may even cuddle women who cry at the drop of a hat, Penny makes men ill at ease when she says things like, "You seem like such a great guy. Why are you interested in me?" One time, after she had a few great dates with a guy one of us set her up with, she turned to him and said, "I know you'll never call me again." Supposedly (according to a friend who reported back the guy's side of the date), Penny spent a good deal of time telling this date how one of her biggest clients had just fired her—because she didn't feel that Penny was motivating enough—and worrying that she would never get another client like that one again.

Although Penny may have some serious underlying issues that require professional help, we have found that her brand of negativity is widespread. More than a few women we know view the pimple on their cheek as catastrophic as skin cancer (and aren't afraid to share this with their date) or think a blind date is the perfect forum to launch into any kind of mistreatment that has affected their lives, leaving their dates frozen in an emotional and physical state known in some male circles as "What the Fuck Am I Supposed to Say to That?"

Many men we know have been on dates with attractive, seemingly together women who, as early as the first date, relay tales of woe, neglect, and violence. Some even went as far as to describe a date rape, and another revealed her prescription meds regimen for depression, anxiety and . . . *schizophrenia!* Unless the guy has the rare disorder wherein he needs to take care of sick or emotionally distressed women, he will usually drop off the woman after the main course never to be heard from again.

Put yourself in the guy's shoes. He's on a date, looking for a great time, and suddenly he has to handle a very delicate situation, with someone who he now thinks may be dangerously unbalanced. The "Poor Me" syndrome can manifest itself later on in relationships, too, when women seek attention (and pity) for any sort of problem (real or embellished), whether it deals with work, friends, family, or otherwise. It's okay to want attention, but not the kind of attention that is based on exaggerated hardship.

It's too bad for Penny that most men are unwilling to take on the charity project that is her self-esteem.

The Antidote   Penny's apparent physical charms are soon overshadowed by her lack of self-confidence, not to mention her disturbing disclosures (like her struggle with eating disorders—a favorite conversation piece of hers). Unless Penny takes some time to reflect on her habit of pushing men away with her downer rap, she'll never truly understand her own responsibility in barely getting past the first few dates.

If you haven't seen a pattern developing, we'll spell it out for you now: Yappers often blame others for their problems because there is too little time for introspection while they're doing all that yapping.

Yapper Syndrome 4: "Ante-It-Up Annie"

Annie is getting her masters in business at an Ivy League university. Good for Annie. She is at the top of her class and, because she's a student of all the fashion magazines as well, she is always stylishly dressed. While not exactly the most, shall we say, *photogenic* of individuals, she straightens and lightens her hair, has plenty of dermatologic treatments, and has bleached her teeth to a pearly white sheen. She has mentioned to us more than a few times her tendency to gain weight, but because that would mean she would have to buy new clothes, which is just not in her annual budget, she tries to moderate her intake of food. Essentially, she makes the most of what she has and the overall impression is that of an attractive and confident woman.

We should also mention that Annie is from a middle-class suburb of Chicago but dreams of a much better life for herself. By any standards, she has achieved a lot thus far by putting herself through college and her postgraduate studies and certainly has our respect in this area. She travels in a fairly well-to-do circle: Many of her girlfriends are successful, have married successful guys, or were born with silver spoons in their mouths. Annie, no doubt, aspires to have all the things her other girlfriends have.

When it comes to men, Annie is attracted only to men who are destined for the Forbes 400. In fact, she once broke up with a premed student she'd dated a few times, who told her he was falling in love with her, after she realized she would have to invest too many years and late nights before he would earn a steady income and be able to pay off his loans (we have our sources). Annie is on the hunt for a rich guy. Go Annie. The problem is that she thinks that if she directly comes out and tells her dates that she wants to find a guy with money, they'll find it refreshingly honest and straightforward. The reality is that for most men it's a complete turnoff.

When she does have a date (prescreened for earning potential), Annie feels she needs to find out whether her date has *drive*, as she calls it, and would be able to give her the kind of life she requires. She has told us that she feels strongly that asking a guy what his goals are is perfectly legitimate conduct. Though that's not a terrible question (although it's about as romantic as a job interview), mutual friends have told us that she can cross the line when she repeats her mantras "Unless a man can give me two carats or more, he might as well not bother" and "I'm too good for a starter anything" or "I will not be seen in an American-made car."

While Annie has every right to think and say these things, she should take a moment to reflect on how she is perceived. Which is, more often than not, as a cold-hearted, shallow snob. They may have started off rich, but none of the successful men we know started off successful. Many of them credit the loving, supportive women behind them as keys to their success (as many of the successful women we know credit their success to the supportive men in their lives).

You'd think Annie would have learned her lesson in college, when she was dating Steve, a self-described computer geek. They really enjoyed each other's company; Annie found that Steve had a quick wit and loved that he spoke several languages. On the third date he made a beautiful gesture of taking a bouquet of daisies to her door. They went to a movie and then for dessert at a local coffee shop, where Annie asked Steve how he defined success and how he would go about achieving it. Steve was hesitant with an answer and tried to change the subject, but Annie would have none of it. Finally, Steve said, "I'm going to do what I love doing and hopefully I'll be successful." Annie made it pretty clear to Steve that she felt their views on success were not the same. It was their last date. When she got home and looked at the daisies that she placed in a vase in her bathroom, she told our mutual friend the next morning, "I could never enjoy a life filled with daisies when I could have something a little more exotic."

You've probably guessed that Steve is a wildly successful dot-com millionaire loaded up the wazoo. You're right. His wazoo is loaded. This experience hasn't changed Annie. She still feels that her line of questioning is wholly appropriate.

The Antidote   It's great to have big dreams for you and your man, but in your effort to close the deal, being vocal about your superficial prerequisites for marriage is not going to help your cause. We can't tell you that it's not that important to marry a rich guy. To some women, financial stability is paramount, and we can understand that. Just don't talk about it so much. Better yet, look beyond his great job or his savings account. Find out whether or not the person is good-natured and has similar *values*. Telling a man what you want or what you deserve isn't going to make him want to give it to you.

Remarketing Your Conversation

BEFORE YOU THINK THIS CHAPTER IS ABOUT only what you shouldn't say, let us change direction for a moment. Let's talk about *how* you say things, which can also be crucial. Everyone has a past, a present, and a future (however long or short). How you address these segments of your life is important to how people perceive you.

Life's twists and turns and how we respond to them are what make us unique. How the twists and turns are packaged is an entirely different story. When you do reveal insights about yourself, why not repackage your past a bit, recycle your present, and forecast an interesting future? We'll call it **Speech Spin** because we had to think of something catchy.

Speech Spin is more useful earlier on in a courtship when the two parties are getting to know each other and every little piece of information can have significant meaning and can influence a relationship. But whether you've been together for a while or are just starting to date, it's never too late to micromanage how you relay any information. In other words, it's not just about what you say but *how* you say it. Speech Spin is another key to being a modern-day Scheherazade, because you can alter what you want to say in the slightest way and come across golden.

To help illustrate the concept of Speech Spin and how to re-market your past, present, and future in everyday conversations, we've recycled some common statements and rephrased them for optimal results.

Speech Spin

Pre: My husband left me after three months and ran off with my best friend.

Post: I was married very young and it just didn't work out.

Pre: I ran into my ex at lunch today, and we grabbed a coffee to catch up on things.

Post: My ex spotted me at a restaurant and attempted to update me on his life, like I still care.

Pre: When you come home after hanging out with your friends you act like you're three years old.

Post: The way you behave when we're alone together makes me so horny.

Pre: Are you dancing or having a seizure?

Post: I would love to take some ballroom dancing classes together.

Pre: When are you going to trade in this old beater for a Beemer?

Post: I am so worried for your safety when you drive in this car. Let's see if we can find something that'll survive a collision with a shopping cart.

Pre: I once had a sick threesome in Club Med.

Post: If you're a good boy, you may be in for a surprise.

Pre: If it's not over two carats, don't bother.

Post: Wow, did you see that woman's ring over there? It's bigger than a Duraflame. Boy, is she lucky.

Pre: I can't believe a guy like you is still interested in little ole me.

Post: I can't say I'm surprised you called, but it *was* great to hear from you.

Pre: You don't know what you're talking about . . .

Post: You have an interesting point, however, I feel . . .

Pre: My old boyfriend is hung like a horse.

Post: I've never met a man quite like you.

Pre: You're not still living at home like a loser, are you?

Post: Do you have roommates?

Pre: I only fly first class.

Post: Did you hear about that study they did where people who flew coach got more blood clots than people who flew first?

Remember, recycling isn't lying. You can give him more details the more you get to know him, but as a modern-day Scheherazade, think about what you actually say and how you say it. When it comes to talking, most men care about quality more than quantity. Use discretion when bringing up sensitive issues. And always remember, you're not on a job interview, you're on a date.

No matter what you take with you from this chapter, try to find your inner Scheherazade. Don't underestimate the importance of discretion, titillation, and patient listening when in the company of your man. This doesn't mean that your boyfriend shouldn't accept you for who you are; it means that monitoring your conversation can only make yourself more attractive. There's no shame in filtering yourself—even the finest wines in the world have to be filtered before they can be consumed. And we'll drink to getting you consumed.

7

Men and Sex: The More We Write About It, the Harder It Is

A NOTE FOR OUR VIRGINAL READERS: BASED on what we know and can explain here, if you're saving yourself for marriage, your future husband will treasure every moment with you. So you can skip this chapter until after you're wed—but we recommend you bone up on the facts sooner than later.

And now for the rest of you: We're sure you're wondering how we are going to condense a topic like sex and relationships into one chapter when other people (like Madonna) need entire books *with* graphic pictures to cover it. But our objective here is to talk about sex as it relates to your relationship when it comes to closing the deal. Among other things, attitudes about sex can differ greatly between men and women and *among* men and women. Since you already know how *you* feel about sex, we don't need to spend any time dissecting *your* attitude. As usual, we will probably offend you at some point, but you should be used to this by now.*

Although our wives had better disagree, we humbly admit that we are not experts in this area. However, we do have a very good idea about how men think about sex in relationships. We will discuss the different issues associated with sex that come up in modern long-term relationships, and our goal is to help you navi-

----

* Please take into consideration that our opinions have been formed by years in fraternities, locker rooms, and of course, bachelor parties, and we can say with some accuracy that we know what men are thinking.

gate this very sensitive subject as you move forward in your relationship. Think of this chapter as the sexual Cliff's Notes to deal closing.

Why Boys Love Chemistry and Erector Sets

WHATEVER THE SCIENTIFIC EXPLANATION for chemistry (i.e., sexual attraction) may be, we couldn't care less. One of us almost failed science. What we do know is that there is a very basic truth: You can love spending time with someone and that person can be great for you, but if neither party is interested in jumping the other's bones, then most likely you'll remain just friends. Chemistry—an earth-moving sexual magnetism—adds up to the same thing: You love the way your partner smells, feels, tastes, looks, etc. All four tactile senses are involved, and you should pay attention to each of them.

We believe that sexual attraction must be innate to the relationship to sustain the romance. Once you move past the attraction, however, things can get complicated. You should always look beyond the sex to what you have as a couple. Just because you've got great chemistry doesn't mean you're meant for each other.

Sexual Compatibility

JUST BECAUSE HIS GENITALS FIT INTO YOURS doesn't mean you two are compatible in bed. Sometimes couples can't seem to get it together in the sack. Having bad sex doesn't mean your relationship is doomed, but it does indicate that you're going to have to work on it.

Can't agree on a comfortable position? He likes the doggie/cowgirl combo and you like it missionary? When two people love each other, enjoy each other's company, and have great chemistry, below-average sex is not something that has to undermine a great relationship.

If you find that sex with your partner is increasingly difficult, boring, uncomfortable, awkward, or anything other than pleasurable, our advice is to talk about it *before* you have it. Don't wait until you're mid-act to bring up that certain positions hurt you or that you weren't ready "for that." Part of great communication is timing. The grounds for *coitus interruptus* shouldn't be *coitus argumentus*. Spend however much time you need, and get as explicit and detailed as you need to. Our advice is to frame the discussion in terms of *what you like or want* rather than *what he's not doing*. After this sensitive conversation, you might suddenly find yourself hyperaware of everything you are doing to each other, but before long you two will be shagging happily like two bunnies.

And one more thing: If your man likes to have sex with other women, you need to learn to accept it. (Kidding! Relax.) The *only* time your sex life is allowed to wane (but remain monogamous) while you're dating is if you're in different countries or there's a sickness or death in the family. Continual bad sex or a loss of attraction or interest by one partner early on is an indicator that the relationship may *not* be the one.

GASP! Generally Accepted Sexual Principles

CAUTION: NO MATTER WHAT ANYONE SAYS, safe sex today is of paramount importance. Many people with HIV/AIDS or STDs may look healthy and not even know they have something. Whether it's using latex condoms or getting tested, it's crucial to be responsible *before* you engage in sex. Also, do note that the fastest-growing segment of the population (according to the *New York Times*) infected with HIV/AIDS is minority *women* and men. The reason we mention this is that for those of you who don't know, it is *no longer* (nor was it ever) exclusive to the gay or drug-using community. Protect yourself.

When to Have It

Half a century after the birth of magazines like *Playboy,* the sexual revolution, and the summer of love, the main issue these days for a vast majority no longer seems to be *whether* to engage in premarital sex, but *when.* Just as you wonder how long you should be together before you contemplate marriage, you may have asked yourself how long you should wait to sleep with him, especially when you're dating a guy you might one day actually marry.

Our general answer to this question is to wait until it feels right—and then wait a little longer. Like that thing you said to your old boss that got you fired, there are certain things in life you can't ever take back, and we'd rather you not regret it. If you find the temptation incredibly difficult, then just remember the following: If this is the guy you *do* end up marrying, in a few years you and he will have a hard time remembering what it was like *not* having sex with each other.

Another reason we feel you should wait is that, whether most men care to admit it, they like to *earn* their sexual conquests. Give it up too freely and your man will wonder who else planted their flag before he did. Of all the men we know and all the men we asked randomly, we couldn't find one who broke up with a girl because she wanted to wait another few weeks or even a month or two. Like the lesson you probably learned in eighth grade that (we believe) all girls should be taught: If he breaks up with you because you're not giving it up, then he doesn't deserve you in the first place. Of course, there *are* great, hot passionate flings that turn into marriage, but this book is about maximizing your odds when it comes to deal closing.

Are we worried that we'll receive threats from men who are trying to get laid? No, because *we* know that *they* know that if they're serious about a girl, they'll secretly hope she's been somewhat discerning about whom she's slept with. While substantive men may ogle strippers, the majority are not looking to raise kids with one. (Please note: If you're reading this for fun and not looking to get married at this very moment, as a gesture of solidarity to our fellow men, we would like to encourage you to keep enjoying your safe one-night stands.)

Most likely you're already sexin' it up with your boyfriend. You just want to know how to keep the love going and keep him happy.

The Delicate Balance

We've overheard locker room conversations similar to this:

George: Hey, Bob, your girlfriend's fuckin' hot, bro.
Bob: Thanks, G.
George: She any good, you know, in bed?
Bob: Amazing.
George: Ever wonder how she got that way?

This exchange happens in locker rooms across the country and around the world daily. It illustrates that many men want their woman to be virginal, but with natural porn-star talent. We call that desire the **Delicate Balance** because they want you to be good in bed but not to the point where they wonder where you trained. The easiest way to maintain the Delicate Balance is by finding out what turns on your boyfriend and following through with it (as long as it doesn't make you uncomfortable). In other words, discover each other's boundaries and forge new ones, but never to the point that you're alienating or ignoring your mate.

While men want their women to be able to pleasure them, they also want to know that they can pleasure their women. Men can also be insecure with the level of their gal's experience. You may find it a bit tenuous, but it's up to you to build up your man's confidence in the sack by not making him feel as if he's just one of the many guys who've enjoyed the pleasure of your company. If you're a tad more practiced than he, this may offset the Delicate Balance.

An example of how to achieve the Delicate Balance might be that when you first start having sex, be good—but not too good. What's wrong with a little more stroking of his ego? If your boyfriend's like most men, it shouldn't be too hard to bring him to climax the first few hundred sexual encounters, anyway. (If you do find it surprisingly difficult, you should immediately run to your local video porn shop and see if you recognize his face on any of the adult film boxes.) You should have to worry about getting him to orgasm only after twenty years of marriage.

Here are a few basic rules that will help you maintain the Delicate Balance:

1. Initially, at least, avoid discussing your sexual history. It's nobody's business and no good can come of it.
2. Be willing to "try anything." (Making him think that it's your first time won't hurt.)
3. If they can get only one thing from you, their general order of preference is: (1) blow job (because there's no effort on their part); (2) sex (he won't care with which part or where); (3) hand job (even though he doesn't do anything here either, it comes third in order of preference because it's so middle school . . . okay, high school).
4. *Don't* bark at him during sex unless you're sure he's the rare kind of guy that likes being told what to do. Just moan when he does something you want more of. He'll catch on quickly.
5. *Do* tell him how great he is. Tell him he's number one! Just don't mention it's out of one hundred.
6. Remember his name (including pet ones).

7. If you're going to talk dirty in the middle of sex, make sure he likes that sort of thing.

8. Suggesting you make a porno together is fine. Suggesting you call your friend who directs all your pornos is not.

9. If he asks to try a new position, don't say you don't like it if you haven't tried it with him yet.

10. If you have a reputation from your vast past sexual experiences and something catches up with you, remember the following three words: *deny, deny, deny.* If a piece of evidence shows up that ties you to the event in question, keep denying until they ask for your DNA, then consult an attorney. While some of you may think this is "lying," we feel it is only if one of the secret situations occurred in the time that you've been with your current boyfriend. What happened at the fraternity with your college boyfriend is still part of your sexual history, and unless there's an STD involved we believe it's no one's business. Remember Scheherazade. Too much honesty can kill or strangle desire. We've seen it happen. While honesty is the best policy, we firmly believe you should tell him only what you're comfortable with. Every experience or fantasy is *not* his business.

Love It (or at Least Like It)

Honestly, there's nothing scarier to a guy than knowing that one day he's going to commit himself to one vagina for the rest of his life. We actually know a few guys who freaked out and walked away from marriage over this. So, how can you help make this transition easier for your man? By selling your vagina! No, not literally. We mean by making your vagina seem extra special. Whether with a bit of creative grooming or encasing it in the prettiest lingerie, make what you have what he wants. And then when you've found out what he likes on you, find out what he likes on him. Make an effort to pinpoint what makes your man happy. Uncover his erogenous zones. If he likes things a certain way and the local sheriff's department is cool with it, then why not try to love it too?

Another thing we're sure he'll like—and you may too: oral. If, through this book, we can make just one woman understand the depth to which men appreciate oral sex, then we have performed an invaluable service to mankind. Whoever coined the phrase "it's better to give than to receive" wasn't receiving oral sex at the time. Please give.

If you're not big on oral sex but are willing to put that selflessly aside to please your man, then good for you and your fellation-ship.* In our opinion, giving pleasure to your partner and getting to know his body and *how he likes it* is paramount. Both of you should be showing how you care about each other in these ways, and oral pleasure is a great way to do this. In other words, try to get over it, if you can. Giving is receiving.

Foreplay

For women, foreplay is like a delicious appetizer before the entrée. For men, it's like the bumper-to-bumper traffic before getting to the restaurant. You may have noticed that men can get into the mood for sex pretty much any time, so you may have correctly concluded that we require very little emotional (read: no) stimulation to get in the mood. We don't need candlelight dinners or flowers. For us, stimulation is a much more visual experience. For example, if we see a Victoria's Secret commercial or billboard, we will think about sex. Many women, on the other hand, need to be lured into the act with conversation and then caressed, kissed, licked, and fondled to get into the mood for sex. Basically, a lot of

* Thanks for the word, Robinne Lee!

you have to feel connected to us in some way. Worse yet, you usually have to actually *like* the guy too.

As much as you may have a problem understanding how one can get turned on so quickly, men have the same problem trying to comprehend why you won't let us just (to put it crudely) *stick it in*. We figure, once we're in there, what's not to like?

We would never suggest that you forgo your foreplay, but we ask that you keep in mind that for many men it can be a laborious step on the way to fulfilling our sexual needs. If you like and desire foreplay, we suggest that you talk about how nice it is rather than complaining about what he's not doing. He'll surely get the message through positive reinforcement. Believe us—men aim to please. (Yes, it's part of the ego thing. You're catching on quickly!)

Remember when you were a kid and you figured out that when you were better behaved it was more likely that your parents were going to spoil you a bit more? That's the spirit in which you should treat foreplay in your relationship. Also, there is nothing wrong with letting him know that since you loved his spending time kissing your neck, he's now in for a special treat. Hey, it works for dog trainers. This way, everyone benefits: You're getting your princess fantasies taken care of and your man still thinks he's the king of your castle.

Pornography

In the following paragraphs we have assumed the following:

1. Your boyfriend enjoys the occasional pornographic indulgence. (You can define *occasional* any way you like, as long as it is relatively normal and healthy; and you can define *relatively* and *healthy* any way you like, as long as you don't have to one day define *indictment* for your boyfriend.)
2. You like pornography less than he does.

Studies, schmudies—we've heard it all when it comes to pornography. There are some studies that conclude that the more men watch pornography, the less they are interested in sex with their partners. We've heard other studies that state pornography is a safe and faithful way to experience alternative fantasies. For our discussion, none of this will matter. It also won't matter whether someone, somewhere, has defined pornography as addictive or destructive to society. The fact is, it exists everywhere, from the Internet to late-night soft porn on mainstream premium cable channels to magazine racks at local airports. People are enjoying all this pornography, and the odds are decent that you might be dating one of them. Of course, we're referring to the legal adult porn stuff . . . not the sick stuff you have to e-mail former Soviet republics to get.

Why do men like pornography? We've already told you that men are greatly stimulated by visual cues. Other than engaging in sex, what could be more stimulating than watching two or more attractive people engaged in sex? The answer for us is *nothing*. Men like pornography because it lets them watch a variety of beautiful women in fantastical situations performing erotic acts and acting (albeit horribly) as if they enjoy it.

If you are bothered by pornography or your man's interest in it, then you need to figure out with your boyfriend what will make both of you comfortable. First question: What's really bothering you? Is it that you are taking his enjoyment of pornography personally? All therapists (we've asked a few) will tell you that fantasies are normal and healthy. Trying to control or deny your partner or yourself an active fantasy life will ultimately be detrimental to you, to him, and to your relationship.

Second question: Does it make you feel insecure about your sexual relationship? If you know your man is getting a woody to the image of a skanky buxom blonde, it certainly doesn't mean he wants to bring her home to Mom or out with the boss. Have confidence and remember that he chose you. Men don't "switch off" their visual fantasy life just because they get married. There will always be those fantasy girls, but you're his fantasy *reality*.

If you think that his liking pornography is causing him to hate sex with you, then the problem isn't with porn, it's with your boyfriend. If your man has a hard time separating the fantasy world of pornography from the reality of your sexual relationship, then you need to discuss more than just the pros and cons of pornography. In either of these instances a frank conversation and a trip to a couples counselor might be in order.

Third question: Do you take issue because you find the material offensive? Your sense of morality is wonderful, but *you're* not him. Just as you may like different movies or prefer a different dish at the Chinese restaurant, don't expect him to feel the same way you do.

It is our opinion that men don't give up pornography any easier than other vices, so if it's really an issue for you, make sure that you're ready with a compelling argument (though probably, to be honest, it won't make a difference). If you're really opposed to it, find a solution that you can both live with, like no pornos when you're around. As always, calm discussion is best. Making your partner feel bad or guilty or giving unreasonable ultimatums is never good for a relationship or deal closing.

Just because your boyfriend likes pornography doesn't mean you have to. But while you may initially be turned off by the idea of your man looking at porn, there also can be a brighter side. *Yes, there's a plus to porn!* Pornos aren't a substitute for sex in a healthy relationship, but in some relationships they are an enhancement to it. In some cases it can be a great thing for you if your man likes porn. Why? Think about all those times *you* aren't in the mood or begging for it. What about when you have your period and/or you're not feeling sexy? What about when he's out of town on business? His fondness for porn can certainly take his mind off things that could be a lot worse for your relationship, like his looking for another (real) woman. Which leads us to . . .

Masturbation

Now you're in the hands of masters.

Let us share some wonderful masturbatory wisdom with you:

1. Your boyfriend's masturbation has very little bearing on the health of your sex life.
2. Men in happy and committed relationships masturbate.
3. We know that some of you probably do it too.
4. It's natural and healthy (sayeth us).
5. It's for (almost) everyone.
6. It's the safest sex around!
7. It can be a source of guilty feelings.
8. It is a great stress reliever.
9. It can enhance sex with your boyfriend.
10. It can lead to hairy palms. (We hope you know we're kidding.)

Personal and religious beliefs usually determine where one stands on the subject of masturbation. It's a safe bet that your boyfriend still masturbates unless he is devoutly religious or is a rare, rare breed. (If he is devoutly religious, then odds are that so are you, so you should have put down this book after reading the jacket.) So, like we said, most likely your boyfriend's a masturbating fiend. Though many of our friends might not admit to masturbating, when we press them under heavy cross-examination, using our patented good cop/bad cop routine, most of them admit to it. The conclusion, then, besides that we need to find new friends, is that masturbation is a force to be reckoned with.

So your boyfriend likes to choke the old chicken, huh? What a pervert! Actually, jerking off is one way your boyfriend can have a private sexual encounter just the way he likes it. He can go as fast or slow as he wants and not think about your feelings. We think you should be open to accepting his desire to masturbate, because either way he's going to do it, and if you're cool with it too, it's just one more thing that you can be supportive of in your role of fabulous, cheerleading gal pal (and future wife).

But why? Why can't he just be satisfied with your most excellent sex life? The truth is that it's more than just being able to do it how and when he wants to. Masturbation has plenty of extra benefits too, some of which apply to *both* of you. Many experts believe that people who masturbate have a better understanding of what gets them excited; they learn how and where they like to be touched. When they share this information with their partners, it can lead to a more fulfilling sexual relationship. Other than $150-an-hour psychotherapy, we can't think of a better way to get to know yourself. Self-actualization is fun!

P.S. According to a study in an article just recently published in the *New York Post,* the more men ejaculate (during sex or masturbation) between the ages of twenty and fifty, the less likely they are to suffer from prostate cancer. The findings were published in the *Journal of the American Medical Association.* So tell your boyfriend to either hop to it—or on you!

Fantasies/Role-Playing

When one of the authors told his wife's grandmother that he was writing this book, she said, "When you get to the sex chapter, you're going to write about fantasies, right?" Then her daughter (his mother-in-law) piped in, "What are some of yours, Mom?" Which prompted him to say, "While you do bring up an excellent point, Granny, I'm going to have to end this conversation right now, before I hear about the sexual fantasies of my daughter's great-grandmother." After all, that wasn't the ideal legacy he was hoping she'd leave for offspring.

That conversation did clear up one thing, however. People have been acting out their sexual fantasies and role-playing for at least as long as one author's grandmother-in-law has. We figured that since this woman had a very proper upbringing, fantasies and role-playing must be more typical than he originally thought, especially if she's willing to talk about it now . . . with her granddaughter's husband! Of course, Granny is a hip, bright woman who understands the benefits of fantasies, especially in a monogamous relationship.

Whether you act out fantasies with medieval maiden/knight, cheerleader/football hero, or librarian/bookworm roles, they all serve the wonderful purpose of keeping things new and fresh. When it comes to sex, new is almost always better, especially for men who, shall we say, have been prolific in their sexual exploits. Sex is as much in the head (the cerebral one) as it is in the body. *Sexuality, sensuality,* and *eroticism* are all mystical words, partially because they're based in fantasy. Having an active fantasy life is part of what's important for couples and for men to keep things hot and bothered. Suppressing or controlling your or your man's fantasies is like putting a damper on someone's dreams and aspirations. Settling down for a monogamous life is generally difficult for men (and women), and fantasies and role-playing can be a healthy and fun way to liven things up—as long as his fantasies do not include a white sequined glove, a surgical mask, and a chimpanzee.

Sexual Issues

Sexual issues come in many shapes and sizes and include a wide variety of problems and symptoms, from not being able to reach orgasm to having an unhealthy body image. The avalanche of sexual imagery and content can be overwhelming; the ridiculous ideals and endless sexual information from magazine articles to television talk shows would give anyone a hang-up. Sometimes too much information is exactly that: too much.

If all this overexposure is undermining your sexual relationship and self-confidence, you may have to take matters into your own hands. (For our purposes we have to assume that whatever it is, it is causing concern for the future of your relationship.) For example, if you are shy about showing yourself to your man because you feel you have a mild case of FASSS (Fat ASS Syndrome), then we can suggest either learning to love yourself (a very sexy thing to do) or doing something that makes you feel better, like going to the gym or skipping dessert. If your man suddenly can't perform, it's probably not because you gained back the freshman fifteen, but maybe that he lost his job, or a parent, or he is having a difficult moment. Whether it's yours or his or both of yours, if it's a more serious issue, it's never too late to seek professional help, especially if you care about your man and salvaging your relationship. Either way, showing him support and understanding will win you kudos—possibly forever.

Since the days of cavemen and hunter-gatherer civilizations, man has taken great pride in his sexual prowess. Anything demoralizing can have lasting effects on a relationship. Our advice is to boost your man's self-confidence, and your caveman will come out swinging! When it comes down to closing the deal, sexual issues need to be addressed at all costs. Monogamous sex is hard enough to swallow. Bad monogamous sex with emotional baggage is unbearable.

There's always a solution, and fixing it together can bring you closer (to being a deal closer). A few of our friends can vouch for this. Let's learn from others.

Jeremy and Lila

JEREMY AND LILA ARE A PRETTY HOT COUPLE. This medical salesman and stylist could be on the covers of fitness magazines. With her *Playboy* body and his ripped abs, you'd think they'd be doing the nasty for Pay-Per-View. Though their sex life was extraordinarily active at the beginning of their relationship, Jeremy had a setback that affected it. When Jeremy lost his job, he also lost his self-confidence. Having to rely on Lila's stylist gigs after three months of looking for work made him feel less than a man.

Days at the gym working out only made him feel more like a failure because he felt like a kept man—a guy who brought nothing to the table and had no other uses except to look good for his woman. Needless to say, anger and resentment built and their sex life withered. Neither of them addressed the issue head-on, and it spiraled out of control.

One night Lila came across a photo of the old "confident" Jeremy, and after some reflection she decided to take action. Lila loved Jeremy, and even with his current problems she could see herself marrying him and wanted to close the deal. Lila planned a weekend to help Jeremy get back his self-confidence, which she felt would help him in the interview process. Instead of complaining that he wasn't contributing to the household bills or that they never went out anymore, Lila cooked a beautiful meal, drew a hot bath, lit candles for him, and called it their forty-eight-hour Home Spa weekend. They spent Saturday locked in their apartment, eating great food, watching reruns, giving each other relaxing nonsexual massages, bonding, and talking about how Jeremy was handling his lack of work. Lila told Jeremy in words and actions that she'd be there for him no matter what and didn't love him for his employment status. Jeremy and Lila reconnected mentally and physically, and each remembered why they were together in the first place.

Jeremy eventually took a job (with a bit of a pay cut), but he was humbled even more by Lila's support and caring. A few months later, Jeremy had a better idea about what to do with his paycheck than paying the rent. He bought a ring.

Sexual High Kinx

Many men fantasize about being with two women at the same time, and many women openly discuss sexual experimentation with partners of the same sex. There's a new form of sexual openness, and it might have seeped into your bedroom. However, we must be honest. We believe bringing another partner into a relationship, especially prior to closing the deal, will complicate things. The people we spoke to who were in serious relationships and had done it told us that the presence of the third party damaged the relationship in some way.

There is a difference between sexual openness and making the leap to a third partner or group situation. While there are couples who enjoy this, we don't believe that this type of behavior is great for closing the deal or keeping it closed. Many people find the complications too much to bear when new feelings (like jealousy) further complicate relationships, which are often already complicated.

Our advice is to never do anything that will make you feel uncomfortable just to please your partner. If your man is pushing you to have sex with another woman (one typical male fantasy), stand your ground—and always suggest an alternative, as compromise is key to a healthy, long-lasting relationship. Why not try some fantasy role-playing to spice things up a bit? It's another way to give him that variety he's always asking for. Whatever you decide, proceed with caution.

Respecting Yourself and Your Partner (Keep It to Yo'self)

What goes on in your bedroom or on your dining room table should stay there. There's just no benefit to sharing your intimate secrets with friends. Besides revealing inappropriate information that circulates about you and your man, this sort of gossip travels at lightning speed and *always* sticks. Why should lesser-known acquaintances have an inside peek into your bedroom? What right do they have to know your boyfriend's triumphs or inadequacies? After all, if one day this man becomes your husband, do you really want the whole town knowing he had a penile implant or takes Viagra to get it up, even for you, the hottie? Of course, keeping things private is difficult to do, as most people lick their chops at the very intimate problems you have with your boyfriend. There may not be a better reality show than watching your sexual relationship with your boyfriend play out before their eyes. Our advice: Keep a lid on it.

Respect also refers to how you treat each other in the privacy of your boudoir. Whether it's plain sex, makeup sex, romantic making-love sex, fun sex, rough sex, or other sex, the best way to go about it is to always be considerate of your partner. If you're taking care of each other, making each other feel comfortable, and enjoying each other, it will always translate into a better, more enjoyable experience.

Enemy of the Sex: Stress

The speed of today's business and social environment has created overscheduled, overstressed, undersexualized couples. "How can we have sex when we're in different cities or different time zones?" a busy executive complained to us recently. Our advice, honestly, is no matter how stressed, tired, or out of it you are, even if you've been together awhile and assume you can just put it off, it's *very important* to have sex and not take it for granted. Everyone loves it better if timing and location are right, but if you're always searching for perfection you might be putting off much-needed intimacy.

Having sex, even phone sex (or just plain saying "I love and miss you") with your partner if you're on a business trip is better than keeping yourself at arm's length. In order to establish intimacy, you *must* have intimate relations. Even having mediocre sex at these times is A-OK, because it's important, not only for the purpose of having sex, which is fun and pleasurable, but for the purpose of reconnecting with each other, to remember why you're together.

The Last Words on Sex

IN THE LONG RUN, PILLOW TALKING, SNUG-gling, spooning, sharing, and laughing are just as important for a happy relationship as the act of sex itself. If you are in tune with each other's emotions and can laugh at your triumphs *and* inadequacies, then you might just find yourself having more and better sex. And who can't get off on *that* concept? Our feeling is that there are three sexual lives in every couple. Yours, his, and the one you share (a virtual *ménage*!). Focusing on all three is crucial, but put the emphasis on the latter. Everyone knows that sharing is the utmost form of caring.

8

The Art of the Bluff: If You Love Someone, Set Him Free

EVERY RELATIONSHIP HAS ITS DEFINING moments. From the time he surprised you on your anniversary with a vacation to Bali to his offensive comment about your "fankles" at the shoe store—the largest and smallest things can leave lasting impressions on any love affair. But none of these moments will be more major than the moment you decide you've had enough of his excuses and head for the hills.

Whether you plan on coming back or not is the difference between the **Bluff** and **Cutting Bait** (which we'll cover in the next chapter). If you still intend to marry this guy and think you can stomach the emotional roller coaster and the reality it could bring, we're going to coach you in engineering the **Perfect Bluff**, which (disclaimer: when used *correctly*) can be a very useful tool in closing the deal.

Be forewarned, however: Bluffing is a last-resort tactic. Some may argue that bluffing is akin to game playing. If we haven't made it clear yet, we are adamantly against playing games in a relationship. We define game playing as a disingenuous action or comment that is performed or made solely to provoke an emotional response (e.g., purposely leaving, in plain sight, an old love letter from your former flame, a famous NFL quarterback). But bluffing is different because it's pushing the negotiation to a head: Either you're getting married or you're out of there. And you have to mean it! This time—ahem—you're not going back to the relationship if it's going to be the same old, same old. The Bluff is a way to give the control back to you so that the relationship decision-making ball is in your court. It also says, "I'm unpredictable," which most men find incredibly sexy. Unless, of course, you're performing surgery on them.

Here's a simple but difficult fact to digest: There is essentially one of two reasons that you're not engaged. Either he doesn't think he's ready or he doesn't think you're the right one for him. The Bluff will work *only* if the reason is that he doesn't think he's ready. If he doesn't think you're the right one, then no matter what you do, the outcome of your relationship isn't lookin' pretty. If you believe it's the latter case, you should turn to Chapter 9 and read how to Cut Bait immediately (that means getting out before your friends have to buy you the large-print edition of this book).

If it's the former and he's told you he's not ready, you must ask yourself, "Am I willing to wait around *no matter* how long it takes for him to be ready?" If you are the proud owner of a spine, the correct answer is "Hell, no!"

The perfect outcome of any bluff, in poker or a relationship, is winning the pot. Nothing will be clearer to you if soon after your bluff the locksmith van pulls up as you load your suitcase into the cab: You didn't have a winning hand. But if it rattles him completely—if it makes him realize how unbearably his new life would suck *sans toi*—then you, yes, you, have just won the pot by executing the Perfect Bluff.

But you must prepare yourself for either outcome, because while you expertly deliver the message that you are not going to stick around forever, he may very well take you up on your offer. Our experience, however, is that most men who are in love come back with their tails between their legs. They become one of the most desirable objects in this book: A Man with a Plan.

Why Bluffs Work

BLUFFS WORK FOR MANY REASONS, BUT none more important than this: While he's busy gathering up the nerve to ask you to marry him, he's become a nervous wreck thinking that you've moved on forever. Or, worse, you're going to sleep with someone he knows. Please note that the Bluff *isn't* about seeing other people. In fact, dating right away can complicate things unnecessarily. Hopefully your man will come around quickly and, if he does, you don't want him to think that the woman whom he was secretly considering marrying a week ago was grinding with some random rebounder at a local bar. That's the kind of thing that gets guys upset enough to do something that might one day end up in a Lifetime movie.

Bluffs also work because if your relationship is even minimally healthy and normal, his life will be completely incomplete when you're gone. In fact, the better girlfriend you've been, the more miserable he'll be. The trusted friend he used to share his lousy workday with is suddenly busy. The dependable date to his boss's house for dinner is outta there. The lover who knows just how he likes it is off somewhere else while he has to get to know his left (or right) hand all over again.

Lastly, this is gonna work because we're gonna teach you how to sell it as if your life depended on it. Which shouldn't be too hard, since at least your happiness does.

Is He Primed for the Bluff?

GOOD PLANNING IS ONLY PART OF PERFECTING the Bluff. Like most things in life, timing is everything, and it's no less crucial here. So, please take the following little quiz about the current status of your relationship to figure out if it's the right time for the Bluff.

1. Have you broken up before?

   If YES, add 1 point. If NO, skip to question 4.

2. Was the cause of any breakup that he couldn't commit?

   If YES, add 1 point. If NO, skip to question 4.

3. Did things change when you got back together?

   If NO, add 1 point.

4. Does he have reason to think you're not a person of your word? (e.g., Have you told him that you're going out with friends only to have him later find you making out with your coworker?)

   If YES, add 1 point.

5. In your estimation, is the relationship at a point where marriage is the next logical step?

   If NO, add 1 point.

6. Have you made it clear to him how you feel about the status of your relationship?

   If NO, add 1 point.

Here's the deal—the lower your point total, the greater the chance that your relationship is ripe for the Bluff. If you've broken up a few times and nothing has changed, then ask yourself why you feel this time it's going to be any different (you might also want to ask yourself why you're still together. Reread Chapter 1 and start paying attention). As far as his believing you're a person of your word, the idea is that if you say you've had enough and you didn't mean it before (and he knew it), then words mean little in your relationship. He might not realize how serious you are about the Bluff until it's too late.

Now let's discuss a thing or two about timing. How long should you two have been dating before bluffing should become a possibility? The short answer is, it doesn't matter. This question is so subjective, it wouldn't be possible to give the same number to everyone. But that's not why it doesn't matter how long you've been dating. Some couples date for a week and stay married for sixty years. Other couples date for twelve years, get married, and are divorced a year later.

Ask ten people how long a couple should be together before marriage should become an issue and you'll get ten different answers. So what's the answer to this question? The answer is to ask an even better question: How much *more* time are you willing to invest in the relationship without getting a commitment from him? Six months? A year? Three years? Six years? When you get tired of waiting, it's been long enough. Since you're the proud owner of *Closing the Deal*, we'll assume your answer is "zip."

You know you've reached the D.I.P., Dating Inflection Point (a moment in time where you must assess your situation), in the relationship when the realities of your situation need to be addressed. There also is a bit of a sliding scale that should be implemented here. For example, four years of a relationship between the ages of eighteen and twenty-two is like spending a year in a relationship when you're between the ages of thirty-six and thirty-eight. By thirty-six, you should be well versed in what works for you.

Just because you have been dating since the seventh cast member of *Friends* was a monkey, it's not necessarily an indication that the relationship is ripe for the Bluff. The length of the relationship, in bluff terms, is meaningless. What matters is that there's a deep, mutual bond between you and your man and that you're fairly confident he'd be miserable without you. The word *fairly* in the previous sentence should *not* be taken lightly. If you're the kind of person who misreads relationship signals, then be methodical here. For example, if you think "yes" means "no," you suck at reading relationship signals.

One friend misread the opportunity to bluff so completely that she went for the Bluff thinking there was a great chance he would be crawling back to her in a few months. Instead, within days, her ex-boyfriend was in another serious relationship. That only made the breakup much more heart-wrenching. So if he's having second thoughts about the relationship anyway, then the

Bluff breakup that you thought was temporary might become permanent. Remember, you have to be prepared for either outcome. We're going to help you increase your chances of getting the outcome you'd like. So let's make sure we tread carefully here.

Things to Consider Before You Bluff

IF YOU BLUFF IN POKER AND YOUR OPPOnent sees your bluff to the end, there's really nothing left to do at that point but admit defeat. And you might not get a chance to win back his money. You are successful with a poker bluff based on your history with your opponents, their faith in their cards, and your ability to deceive. If your opponent can't figure out whether you really do have good cards, then your bluffing chances greatly increase. In other words, you've got to get your opponent to *believe* you're serious.

If, recently, things have been moving forward in the relationship, bluffing may not be the right move. Marriage Momentum comes in many shapes and sizes but is best measured by your past experience. If suddenly he's using phrases like "when we have a family" it may not be the right time to go for the Bluff. On the contrary, if he's made promises that he hasn't kept, then he's apparently *not* A Man with a Plan.

Another issue related to timing is his current circumstance and disposition. Was he recently laid off? Is he currently mourning his childhood dog? Leaving at a bad time could make you appear uncaring instead of principled and confident. The worst message you could send is that you're out the door when things get rocky. Not only won't you accomplish your goal, but you probably won't hear from him after the Bluff.

Put a Clock on It

It's always crucial to be clear about your feelings and what you desire. In this day and age there are plenty of women who don't want marriage or a family and many who do. Men aren't mind readers, so the first step is making sure he is clear about your wishes. Once you've established (to him) that you are one of those women who wants to get hitched, it's time to put your own personal timetable on the relationship. In the movie business, when making a thriller, this process is called "putting a clock on it" and usually refers to the idea that if something doesn't happen by a certain point, there *will* be major consequences. Now, we have to stress that this *doesn't* mean giving ultimatums. Ultimatums are aggressive and have a tendency to put men on the defensive. This process is about finding clarity and moving forward in your relationship. When you do put a clock on it, it's really important that *you* come up with a date that *you* think is fair. As we said in Chapter 2, there is no universal number that you can plug in to the "When is enough enough?" equation. As long as *you* feel that you have settled on a reasonable "getting to know you" stage, you're already halfway there.

Setting the Stage

Packing up your shit and leaving is one clear way to say, "I'm packing up my shit and leaving." That's not the way the Bluff works.

Bluffing should come from a positive, confident place. It's a culmination of careful planning as well as smart execution. While you're breaking up, the underlying message you will be delivering is "I love you, but since you're not ready to commit, let's take a break. If you figure it all out soon and you're ready to get engaged, hopefully I'll still be available." Essentially, the message is that while you're gone he needs to think things through and decide if he's ready to move on to the next step.

Enough with theory—let's talk about application.

The Bluff Checklist

○ Think about your relationship and its history. If it'll help you remember, write down past examples of failed promises, including his not keeping to a timetable or not changing certain behavior. For example, if he told you that the one thing holding him back from buying a ring was his December bonus (and it was a banner year on Wall Street) and it's now April, then put that at the top of the list. One woman we know, whose boyfriend told her for a year that a ring was imminent, pulled the bluff on February 15, the day after Valentine's Day, after he blew another chance to redeem himself. The last thing he was expecting from his girlfriend was the boot. When he finally came to his senses a few months later, he was A Man with a Plan.

We're going to get into the actual conversation you two need to have a bit later in the chapter, but remember, it's hard to argue without specific examples, and since most men don't have the part of the brain that can freely call up good examples at the spur of the moment, you'll probably make your point unchallenged while he stumbles over his words.

○ Spend some alone time and think about what's at stake. This is serious stuff, ladies. When you deliver the who, what, where, when, and how of your bluff, don't ever lose sight of the end goal: You've already made up *your* mind that this is the guy you want to marry. The Bluff is about getting him to make up *his* mind too.

○ Once you execute your bluff, it's also important to have a support group ready to help you through the first few weeks. Make sure that your best girlfriends aren't taking off to the yoga retreat in Mexico without cell phones the week you're going through the Bluff. After all, you may want someone to sit around in your panties with and cry. (Well, at least we like to picture it that way.)

○ Feel confident in your decision. You'll need to convey that confidence while you're giving the Bluff. You may want to spend the week listening to Tony Robbins tapes to gain that kick-ass outlook, but feeling really good about yourself is a key part of the Bluff. This will enhance the assertive tone when it comes to the actual time to face "the" conversation. If you're not *feeling it* before the conversation and not convinced it will go well, don't pull the trigger. Get to the bottom of your self-doubt. Don't look for answers in just yourself; look at your relationship as well. If you're not feeling confident because your boyfriend hasn't made you feel that way, then that should give you even more confidence that you're doing the right thing!

○ Look great. Leaving at the top of your game sends the message that you're a prize. Let him remember how great you looked when you walked out that door. Don't bluff while you're all teary-eyed or looking ragged after a long day at work. A great tip from one of our wives is to look sexy when you know you're going to fight (or bluff), because, and we quote, "Why should he see some ugly hag screaming at him when he can get yelled at by a sexy woman with ruby red lips and know he's not going to get any?" Take that from a deal closer.

Now close your eyes and envision how you want the **Conversation** to go. Lose the rearview mirror, because there's no looking back.

The Conversation

It all boils down to this. You've made up your mind. You've set the stage. Now it's time to act. Let's get into the Five Ws:

Who: Just you and him. Not within earshot of another human soul. The things that come up in this conversation could be terribly private and embarrassing. Put Rover in the bathroom. Turn your cell phone off. Make sure no one else is in the house. There should be no distractions.

Where: Privately and where you can concentrate (i.e., not in a restaurant where a waiter can interrupt or people can overhear you, or in a car where it's easy to get distracted). You can do it wherever you want, but we recommend that you have the Conversation at his place (assuming he doesn't live with his parents) because when it's all over, you can take your things and leave. It's much easier—and more dramatic—for you to walk out the door than it is to push him out. Also, the image of your ass waving good-bye will stay with him for a good long while.

When: We assume you've read the portion on timing. If not, stop skimming this book. Remember not to do it if he's going through a crisis. Also, bluffing right before a long-standing date or important event (like his sister's wedding) is too risky as it will most likely take the focus of the discussion from why you're leaving the relationship to how you could be so cruel to leave him in the lurch (according to his family). Bluffing at or before a family function is more like game playing and should not be done if you want to get real results.

What: Get to the point quickly. Don't give him a chance to get angry or cut the conversation short. Don't let him wonder where you are going with your "little speech." After all, nothing is more annoying than reading an editorial and not knowing what point the writer was trying to make after you've read the entire piece. In your own words, tell him right away that you want to take a break. Then tell him . . .

Why: This must come from your heart. Make sure he knows that this is something you've thought about for a long time and not an emotional response to anything he's done or said in the past day or the celebrity wedding you watched on E! or saw pictures of in *Star*. Tell him that you've waited patiently and that things aren't moving fast enough. Tell him all the reasons that you think you two should be together forever and how you hope he can reconsider his timing before it's too late.

How (the sixth of the Five Ws):   First, be sensitive and understanding to the fact that he probably doesn't want to break up. Comments like "Welcome to Dumpsville—Population: You" aren't appropriate. Make sure to keep things friendly and calm. You also need to communicate that this relationship may be over forever. In fact, if you're a true risk taker, you should tell him that you're pretty sure it *is* already over because you don't think he's capable of turning this around. This may sound like Reverse Psychology 101 to you (it is), but this kind of reasoning has been known to work. If you're not prepared to say this, then you're not prepared for the reality that the relationship may very well be *over*.

THE FINAL COUP DE GRACE—and one that will echo in his mind for the next few weeks (and you can't say this unless you really mean it, ladies!)—is that it's *not* just about the ring anymore. You're upset about all the wasted time and you need some time to get over all the resentment you're feeling.

The Dating Issue

When you are bluffing it is likely that the subject of dating will come up. He may ask you if you're planning on seeing other people or he may assume that you have something lined up and that this is the true motive for your wanting to break things off. However it comes up, we feel that your response should be that you have no plans to date initially, but when you feel up to it you just might go for it. If this is a sensitive point for him, then that's a great sign. In order to make him comfortable, you can tell him that you're breaking up for the right reasons and say, "I don't have any dating plans," in a noncommittal sort of way. You know, like the way he's treated you for the last year and a half.

Walking Out the Door

- Tell your boyfriend that you don't want to speak for a while. Ask him to respect that—and you should too. The time without seeing or speaking to him will help make this easier on both of you. Once the initial emotions die down, you'll both be thinking more clearly about what feels right. Making yourself available to him immediately won't have the desired effect of Life Without You, not to mention that most guys we know are pretty good at talking their way right back in after a breakup like this. Not speaking to him will make you all powerful against this force.

- Don't try any last-minute jealousy ploys like bringing up other men or telling him how much better you'll feel now. Keep it positive.

- No long good-byes and no tears! You're the one in control here. This is not the time for tantrums. There should be nothing left to discuss. It's now time to leave. By the way, leave the drama to the movies. Don't open the door, turn around, and say, "I'm really leaving this time. This isn't a joke. I'm serious. I'm really leaving." There's only one word to keep in mind: *dignity.* Dig it?

The Next Few Days/Weeks/Months

EVERYTHING YOU DO DURING THIS TIME period counts toward your final grade. How you behave now is just as important in determining the outcome of the Bluff. The maturity and restraint you'll display here will be a sign of your true character. Respect yourself and give yourself time to clear and soothe your head. Do not make any big resolutions or big speeches during this time (i.e., telling your coworker what you really think of him or her, since you're on a roll). This is a time for reflection and healing.

If he tries to contact you, tell your boyfriend that you don't want to speak for at least a few weeks. (When asked, most self-respecting bluffers will say that a week is the *absolute minimum*.) Do not take his calls or call him. You've asked him to respect your space, so do the same for him. When you absolutely agree to cut off contact with each other for the duration, stick to it. Every day gets easier.

Don't go out on any dates until you are ready. That includes feeling up to it as well as dealing with possible consequences. Trust your instincts here. If after a little while you want to go out with a group of friends, that's okay. But remember, if he's thinking about getting back together with you as A Man with a Plan, you are being watched.

You must not be the one to reinitiate contact. If your boyfriend wants to pursue a friendship and you're ready to do that, great, but be clear with each other and yourselves what you *really want* from each other. The only reason to get back together with your boyfriend as a couple is if he's A Man with a Plan. Give him as long as he wants, but don't let that stop you from pursuing your own happiness. If he comes back to you in a few weeks or months and you're still single, great. Let him worry about the consequences of his own behavior.

We know that performing and executing a great bluff seems

like a lot to think about. It's really not as complicated as it seems. It certainly wasn't for our friend Cara.

Cara's Story

CARA IS A VERY PRETTY, FUNKY WOMAN who was raised in a traditional Southern family. She has two very protective older brothers and she's very close to her dad since her mother passed away when she was a teenager. After a year living in Boston, where she attended college, Cara moved to Atlanta, where she has worked her way up in a sports marketing firm. While attending an industry event, she met David, a professional athlete who lives in Atlanta as well. A love affair quickly heated up, and Cara fell hard for David; he was exactly the kind of guy she liked: tall, dark, and handsome. He also had a great physique and a terrific sense of humor.

Cara knew at the outset of their relationship that David had a reputation as a partier and a womanizer. It came with the territory of being a sports star, and his being on the road often didn't help matters either. While her friends were somewhat skeptical, Cara went with her gut instinct and jumped headfirst into the relationship. For his part, David was struck by Cara's kind nature and incredible smile (she kind of has a Meg Ryan thing going on) and liked that she was as passionate about her career as she was in bed. Their professional and personal lives were also well matched and seemed to fit like a puzzle. Cara had a real interest in sports and knew a ton about the subject, so their conversations never fizzled.

Like most men, David got shit from his friends and some teammates who alternately tried to disparage Cara and hit on her, partly because David now went out less frequently with them and partly because a few of them were floundering in their own personal lives. Cara knew how his friends felt about her (which was not a great move on David's part). Regardless of the drama, after eighteen months, Cara started to think about settling down and starting a family. One thing no one could accuse Cara of was being shy when it came to letting people know about her personal plans and goals. She was 100 percent up front about her desire to eventually have kids and a family, more so than normal, perhaps because her mother's death had left a void in her life. While she really loved David, she was not the kind of girl who was about to settle for being strung along. She also had anxiety because she sensed that David did not want to be the first of his friends to break away from the pack and become engaged.

Cara was pretty sure that David was monogamous when he was on the road, and he was always telling her how much he loved her. She felt the relationship had been very serious for a long time, and it was certainly portrayed in the local media as such. Whenever she brought up the subject of getting engaged, David would give Cara a big hug and tell her that the time would soon be right and that he couldn't think of anyone who would make him happier. That made Cara feel wonderful. For a while.

Over the December holidays, Cara thought about how she wanted to approach her situation. She truly loved and adored David. She thought they were a great match, as did her brothers, who were crazy about him (and the free tickets). Cara's inner voice told her, as did her Aunt Bea, that she not only *needed* to make a move, but *had* to in order to find out if she and David were really on the road to engagement. She wasn't getting any younger, even though she was in love.

Cara came to one of us and asked what she should do. She and David were scheduled to go to Orlando for a vacation, and she felt that if she went on the trip she was sending him a message that she was okay with everything. After relaying all the gory details, Cara said she was ready to give him an ultimatum. "We know each other well, we get along great, what else is there?" she asked one of us. Well, as you know, we're not fans of ultimatums, so one of us asked Cara a couple of tough questions; mainly, if David knew how Cara felt about the relationship and that she wanted to become engaged. Cara explained that David had told her they'd be engaged "soon," but that was almost a year before and they were still just dating. After going through all the prerequisites, it was clear that we felt Cara's relationship was ripe for the Bluff.

Hopefully it's clear that the Bluff (once again) isn't about game playing. It's about really choosing to end a relationship because you can't go on without a commitment. Cara really wanted to spend the rest of her life with David, but she was also prepared not to. And now back to our story . . .

Cara met David at his home and told him that their time together had been wonderful, and as he'd known for the past few months she'd been expecting some sense of impending commitment. She felt that a year was a perfectly normal "getting to know you" period and she was not about to wait any longer. Cara felt that their relationship was as strong as they could hope for, and she also wanted to start a family soon. David was upset and conflicted. This didn't come out of the blue for him, but he still didn't think he was ready for a wedding. What would his friends and teammates say?

Cara laid it all out on the line for David. She was in love with him and she could see them together forever. But Cara said she had too much self-respect to just sit around and wait for something that may or may not happen. She suggested that David take some time to think about the situation and decide what he wanted to do. Cara said she'd be waiting for him, but not forever. Yes, she was leaving, but the ball was in his court.

After Cara left his house, David called a few of his closest friends on the team (not the guys who had asked for Cara's phone number) for advice. They all said, "Why *should* you compromise? You're only twenty-eight. After all, there are plenty of fish in the sea, especially for a guy like you." (Remember when we said women don't always give other women the best advice? The same can be said of men.)

David gave it some thought and ended up going to Orlando

with one of his best friends. He didn't want to admit (though he did later) that he would rather have gone with Cara, so he put up a good front. Though David had thought he missed being single, after a few weeks of partying, he wasn't so sure. Truthfully, three months into his newfound singledom, David had to admit he was miserable. None of the girls he met could hold a candle to Cara.

For her part, Cara cried herself to sleep for a few weeks but eventually put on a brave face and started dating. As time went on she was actually surprised that she met one or two guys she kind of liked. Not that there was the same spark as she had with David, but she was enjoying herself and willing to put the time into finding her soul mate. Sure, having kids was important to her, but finding the right guy to have them with and to be their father came first. She even invited one of the guys to a PR event she was hosting, as her date. As fate would have it, no sooner did she walk into the event with the new guy than she spotted David out of the corner of her eye, spotting her. She froze for a moment and then turned away. No sooner did David see her turning away (with a date, no less) than he approached her and told her he missed her and that he'd come to the event because he knew she'd be there. Sparks flew. Not only did David realize how much he cared for Cara, but also the separation proved that he was willing to make his own move with or without the consent of his friends.

It was a successful bluff, all right. Today, Cara and David are happily married and have a beautiful son. Sadly, many of David's advisers/best buds are still single and searching.

Working the Bluff

IN THE BLUFF, AS IN LIFE, THERE ARE NO guarantees. Even the most well-executed bluff can permanently end a relationship. That's not necessarily a bad thing, especially when that relationship was probably ending anyway—only a few wasted *years* later. That's probably the greatest benefit of the Bluff: good news or bad, it is a time saver. It forces the couple to assess the status of the relationship when one of the parties (who is certainly entitled to know where she stands) wishes to assess it.

And last, the Bluff can be a girl's best friend, especially when you bluff like there's no tomorrow.

9 Cutting Bait

WE'VE ALL HEARD SOME VERSION OF THE urban legend about the really nice girl who worked two jobs to put her boyfriend through medical school, then five years later, at his graduation, he breaks the news that he's in love and marrying an intern he met in class. You probably think this urban legend isn't true. You're wrong. One of us actually knows her.

"How did this happen?" we wonder. "Didn't she see the signals?" After all, the girl wasted time and money on this creep without appreciation, and now she's right back where she started five years ago, and that place is *nowhere*, except this time she's got a battered ego, a busted bank account, and six more years of undeserved mileage on her wrinklometer. To make matters worse, she has to deal with people around her who keep asking, "Why did you stay in that relationship so long? Why didn't you realize long ago this was going to happen?" These questions are not only irritating and callous, but also excruciatingly painful for people who languish for years in dead-end relationships. Perhaps deep down they probably knew all along they should have left, and now blame themselves for not listening to their inner voice. So now they're stuck with the double whammy: the pain of breaking up after many years together *and* the knowledge that they have some culpability as well. Did we mention our friend's frustration at blowing a multitude of true romantic opportunities that may have presented themselves along the way when she wore a thong that was two sizes smaller? Perhaps we just did.

Cutting Bait is the final and most painful part of any relationship. Leaving a long-term relationship with a significant other can be as difficult and disruptive to many people as filing for divorce. However, leave you must! Don't become the protagonist in your own urban legend.

Don't Let the Door Hit You on the Way Out

YOUR EXIT IN THIS CHAPTER IS DIFFERENT from the one in "The Art of the Bluff" because now there's no looking forward to his possible triumphant return. In *this* chapter, leaving means *leaving*. For good. Think somewhere between "Lose my number" and "I'm serving you with a restraining order." This behavior may seem drastic, but that's because it is. It's over. Poof, be gone!

Redefining the relationship isn't the same as leaving. Having a boyfriend on the side or signing up with a computer dating service doesn't mean you've said good-bye for good. Sneaking away on a blind date or taking a vacation with a girlfriend to a "Hedonism" resort while your boyfriend thinks you're on a business trip doesn't either. Cutting Bait means exactly what it means in the sport (yes, sport) of fishing: the act of severing all ties to an object of desire. And, in this case, with the added hope of throwing the line back in and catching a keeper.

Check Yourself Before You Wreck Yourself

FIRST THINGS FIRST. BEFORE YOU MAKE A decision that will completely change your life forever, evaluate the signs that are indigenous to almost every relationship. They're often difficult to see unless you are looking for them, but once you start the process, you'll be wondering why you didn't see them earlier. It might be because you're too busy and you're not looking often enough, but most likely it's that you are no longer able to be objective about where you stand in this relationship. So grab a friend and evaluate your relationship over a shot of espresso and a dose of reality.

Length   Once again, the amount of time you've put into the relationship is unimportant. It's all about how much *more time* you're willing to give. But we know you are *dying* for a number, so we'll give you one. You should consider getting ready to Cut Bait if you've been in Marriage Momentum mode for more than a year—and you've tried or considered the Bluff—and nothing is happening. Another good benchmark is that if you find a photo of him in bed with his secretary and you couldn't care less, you're ready to Cut Bait.

Fair Play   When thinking about these issues, it's important to remember that men and women have different biological and social clocks. We feel there should be a level of fair play involved when a man dates a woman. Taking up too much of a woman's time without concern for her needs and desires (whatever they may be) is just plain wrong. Frankly, we think it's a really shitty thing to do to a woman. If you have been discussing marriage for an extended period of time and have nothing to show for it, you may very well be on an endless journey.

Age   Does age play a factor in Cutting Bait? For women and men, age comes with different layers of needs and responsibilities. A twenty-something college student has different pressures than a forty-something businesswoman who has an elderly parent, for example. Since a woman who is thirty-nine has a different Dating Inflection Point than a woman who is twenty-two, we'll cover age here for the over-thirty crowd. Generally, if you're in your twenties, age isn't a major factor in Cutting Bait. There's plenty of time to regroup and start over. Age, however, can be important for two major reasons: one, you might want kids; two, you might not want to spend the rest of your life flying solo.

If having kids is important to you and a goal, you're around thirty-five or older, and you're dating a guy who isn't talking marriage, then Cutting Bait is something you should take very seriously. Having children at thirty-seven is fine if you are sure you'll be able to get pregnant, but not everyone *can* have natural children later in life. We believe that the news media has given too much (false) hope to women as they focus on the one or two celebrities who have had successful pregnancies in their late thirties and forties. They rarely focus on the majority of women who have difficulties getting pregnant. Also, it can be dangerous as well as costly to have children later in life. Of course, there are other options. Whatever you decide, that's great, just as long as your decision is based in reality.

Successful deal closers we know have a great understanding of the *value* of time and age. The ones who had Cut Bait in earlier relationships had the confidence to walk away when their boyfriends made it obvious that they had little respect for the idea that time is a valuable and fleeting commodity. As one of our dear mothers once said, "The days go slow, the years go fast." When you're shopping in the Department Store of Time, there are no refunds or exchanges.

One recently successful deal closer and friend Cut Bait twice in her thirties. She found herself in two lengthy relationships (both more than a year and a half long) and Cut Bait after she realized that things were not heading in the right direction (she seemed to attract guys with Commitia). She closed the deal in her late thirties but says that even if she hadn't married, she would have felt better about herself for calling her own shots.

Fear Are you afraid of being alone? Are you telling yourself you'd rather meet someone else (or have another prospect in mind) before you give your current flame the heave-ho? Let's address the *fear* issue: the fear of being alone, the fear of never meeting someone else.

Fear can be self-perpetuating. When FDR said, "The only

thing to fear is fear itself," he wasn't talking about breaking up with your boyfriend, but he may as well have been. Fear has no place in a relationship, especially when ending one. If the only thing stopping you from breaking up is fear of the unknown—like life after your boyfriend—then give yourself a little more credit that you're doing the right thing. It takes a lot of courage to realize that you need to end a relationship. Be confident that your decision is the right one.

Just because you've been in a relationship for an extended period of time, don't undermine your self-confidence. After only a short while you'll realize just how easy it is to slip back into single mode. Given some time to readjust to their new social status, many of the women we know who Cut Bait picked up right where they left off—after only a few weeks of mourning.

On another note, being alone doesn't make you any less attractive to men. Sure, they might question initially why a great girl like you is single, but most men get past that pretty quickly. Some women believe they're more "attractive" to others (or think they have more going for them) when they're in a relationship, like Jillian the Underdater. (We don't think it makes a difference. We also think that shopping around while you're in a relationship sends out the message that you're not a trustworthy individual.)

If you are confident that you've given the relationship your all and/or that you have nothing left to give, then what you *really* should fear isn't being alone. You should fear that you're going to leave after too much damage has been done to *you*. It's understandable if you leave a relationship with emotional baggage— just don't pack those bags yourself.

Somewhere or Nowhere Want to know if you're heading for Splitsville? Ask yourself "Is the relationship I'm in heading *somewhere* or *nowhere*?" Only you can answer this question, but we do provide this handy-dandy chart that will point you in the right direction.

SOMEWHERE

1. He bought you flowers and wrote you a very personal love message on Valentine's Day.

2. He cut his business trip short to see you.

3. He goes to bachelor parties only out of obligation.

4. He thinks everyone wants to date you.

5. He says he could see you having his children.

NOWHERE

1. All you got on Valentine's Day was VD.

2. He schedules a business meeting every Saturday night.

3. He organizes bachelor parties but claims he has no organizational skills when it comes to your birthday or vacations.

4. He gives out your number to his friends in case they might be feeling lonely when they are in from out of town.

5. He looks into your eyes when he says he hates kids and is thinking about getting a vasectomy.

Sometimes it's difficult to see where your relationship is at. For many reasons you may not be able to evaluate the reality of your situation. Distortion is a common problem in many relationships. Are you dwelling on the one nice thing he did for you three years ago while you disregard his recent actions and motives? Or are you realistic in your view of the relationship? Give yourself some hard questions to answer, and you will know whether the relationship is on its way to somewhere or nowhere. Take our friend Janice, for example.

Janice

JANICE IS A SMART, ATTRACTIVE PERSON who is wonderful at giving other people advice. It's her own decisions that are somewhat perplexing. Janice met Seth, an investment banker, five years ago, and was convinced that he was the love of her life. They had a deep connection on every level, but why was she unwilling to see that while Seth took companies public every day, he never did the same for their relationship? A few years into the relationship, Janice had met Seth's parents only once, at the airport, when they asked him at the last minute to pick them up. Seth's favorite excuse was that he didn't really enjoy spending time with his parents and that he was saving Janice from all the drama. Janice took this at face value for a few years but soon realized that for a guy who claimed not to enjoy being around his parents all that much, Seth was spending an awful lot of time with them, especially when he could have been with her.

Janice kept telling herself that they had a wonderful relationship, which was partly true, but Janice never faced facts that it was underground and going nowhere fast. They spent a lot of time together and were very close, but Janice didn't feel as though Seth was looking to get closer. And whenever Janice broached the subject of marriage, Seth would groan and say that she was taking the spontaneity and romance out of the process. Janice was really hoping that she was misreading the signs and that there *was* some

Marriage Momentum, but soon it became all too apparent to Janice that she was looking for an outcome that didn't seem likely.

When Janice finally confronted Seth about the differences between his story and what she perceived to be the truth, Seth insisted that he loved Janice and that moving forward in their relationship had nothing to do with his family. Janice let the issue go a while longer, and even tried to make plans with Seth and his parents, but Seth didn't welcome Janice's efforts at all. She knew that she had to make a tough decision.

Janice never found out whether Seth was using his parents as an excuse or not, but in the end, she realized it didn't really matter. She knew that it was time to Cut Bait because during their time together there was no forward momentum. Janice ended the relationship when she decided she'd had enough and forced herself to take an honest look at where she stood in his life. On the positive side, Janice says, she was in her twenties then, and so she doesn't regret a minute of the time she and Seth spent together. When she saw the fish wasn't a keeper, she got out her knife and cut the line.

Other Signs It's Time to Cut Bait

CERTAIN PEOPLE MAY ALSO REQUIRE MORE *obvious* signs to see if they need to get the bait cutters out. Others need a kick in the pants once in a while. Looking to family or friends is one option. Very often people close to you send off signals that some bait cutting is in order. Is Aunt Sally rolling her eyes when she sees you two dancing at family events? (Granted, Aunt Sally might roll her eyes at your engagement party too, so be sure to take into account the level of bitterness from any family member or friend who reacts verbally or with facial gestures.) Look to the ones who really have your best interests at heart. One woman we know has been in the same relationship on and off for so many years that people have *stopped* asking when she's going to take the next step.

Listen to good friends and relatives, and don't stick your head in the sand. While you may not want to listen to your single, attractive girlfriend who has the hots for your man, you should be on the lookout for even the subtlest of hints from people who care about you. Listen to your married girlfriends or aunts who want nothing more than for you to join the club.

How and Where to Cut Bait

UNLIKE THE BLUFF CHAPTER, IT DOESN'T matter how you look. In fact, if you find yourself thinking about getting all dolled up, then either you're in Bluff mode or you're still deluding yourself that you can change him and that he doesn't have Commitia. That's not to say that you can't leave him with a lasting impression of your beauty; it's just that it's not imperative, and if you find yourself really wanting to look great, you should take another look at where you stand.

This time, breaking up in public isn't such a bad idea. Give yourself options if things aren't going the way you planned it. If voices are raised, if things take a turn for the worse, or if he's making a scene, you can always get up and leave.

What to Say

Be direct. Use **PNP** in all your conversations but especially when you Cut Bait. PNP is an acronym for Positive-Negative-Positive. First, say something positive like "You know how much I loved you and how much I loved the time we spent together." Then the negative: "However, it's been three and a half years, and clearly this relationship isn't going anywhere. So I think it's best that we not see each other anymore." Then wrap it all up in a positive way, "Clearly, it will be difficult, and I'm going to have a hard time moving on." Just stay away from the details. Unlike the Bluff, wherein you spend time outlining what went wrong, when you're Cutting Bait it's just not necessary to leave him with something to think about. It's not worth rehashing what went wrong if you're not interested in fixing it. You may be familiar with the acronym KISS, Keep It Simple, Stupid. It should be applied to the delicate art of telling your boyfriend to kiss off.

Tying Up Loose Ends

SOMETIMES IT'S MORE PAINFUL TO CUT BAIT with your lover because you must also Cut Bait with a member of his family to whom you have grown particularly close. It may be a doting aunt or uncle, a loveable grandma, or terrific parents, not to mention a cuddly kid. While it is heartbreaking for you to walk away from Jim or Bob, it may also be upsetting to know you'll never again see this treasured member of his family.

How should you handle this? If the feelings are strong enough, a well-written note or poignant phone call is always a classy move. Of course, you should *never* involve them in your relationship woes or talk smack about their relative, your ex. A simple "I'm sorry the relationship did not work out, but I wanted to let you know how much getting to know you meant to me and how much you will be missed" will do the trick.

The hardest situation always involves young children or adolescents who are in critical stages of development. It may be very hard on them as well, especially if you are not the first person to whom they have been introduced; they might see these departures as a personal failure. Special attention must be paid here by both parties to make sure the child does *not* see this relationship failure as their fault. If you have bonded with the child, a discussion may actually be warranted, and depending on the level of closeness between you, your ability to assure the child that you are their friend and accessible by phone or by note is a lovely gesture too.

You Cut? Talk It Up!

ONCE YOU FINALLY CUT BAIT, DON'T HIDE under a rock. It's time to broadcast the news among your support system of friends, business associates, and relatives. Although the timing doesn't make it easy, seasoned bait cutters will tell you that being fresh on the market is perhaps the most *fertile* time for fix-ups. Having friends say to a potential prospect "She just broke up with her boyfriend of three years" is not only attractive to men but also newsworthy in dating circles. Men will like the idea that you haven't been single in a while, especially since they won't have to worry about running into any of your recent dates because you haven't had any. You may find yourself surrounded by an old admirer or your cousin's boyfriend's brother who just moved to town.

You may not *feel* like going out, but do know that no matter how long you wait to go out on the town, it won't be any easier. Ripping the Band-Aid off quickly may hurt more at first, but the pain doesn't last as long. Life is funny this way. Don't think we're advocating a rebound relationship, but there's nothing wrong with taking full advantage of new opportunities that may suddenly be available to you. While your ex is drowning his sorrows at a strip joint nearby, you'll be busy creating opportunities.

Too many bait cutters demur and think the initial tidal wave of dates and interest will last forever, and it might. But while many people offer to fix people up, they often don't do the same when your breakup is old news or their sympathy has waned. Fact is, human nature often dictates the old adage "Out of sight, out of mind." Like it or not, people just don't always extend themselves over long periods of time.

Cutting Bait as an Icebreaker

ONCE YOU'RE SMART ENOUGH TO ACCEPT that rebound date, there's nothing wrong with letting him know right off the bat that you've just Cut Bait. We've heard from plenty of our female friends that if you put the right spin on it, he'll feel he's with a winner—someone who has standards, someone who can make a decision, someone who will eventually Cut Bait on him if he doesn't measure up.

Saying something like "I'm sorry if I'm a little nervous tonight. I was in a long-term relationship and this is my first date since I broke up with my boyfriend" is one way to do it. No more, no less. Whatever you do, do not spend the entire evening talking about your old relationship. Be mysterious. Think Scheherazade! Do *not* talk about what went wrong. Do *not* talk about what went wrong. No, we don't have a bad editor. We repeat it because it's a fundamental error people make. Just have a nice time and let him relish the fact that he, Mr. Maybe-A-Keeper, is with a bona fide Grade-A bait cutter!

So I've Cut Bait—Now Look What You Made Me Do!

LIGHTEN UP. YOU JUST SWALLOWED SOME strong medicine and you're going to feel better pretty soon. Take some time and evaluate the mistakes you (yes, you) made in your relationship. Ask yourself *why* and pinpoint *when* the relationship stalled, then make a mental note of the answer and commit to never letting it happen again. You're entitled to mourn the loss of a boyfriend for a while, but not longer than the time between two haircuts.

Cutting Bait is no easier than dumping a dot-com stock after you've held on to it for so long—through the good and the bad. You may feel stupid, angry, and upset. But there's always a bright side to everything! Yes, you're going to have some painful weeks

ahead of you, but no one ever said it's easy. If you subscribe to the philosophy that when you commit to something in life you must commit to it entirely, then you will find it's no different here. You must commit entirely to ending your commitment.

The good news is that things will eventually start looking up. If you keep an open mind and are willing to take a few risks, you might even be surprised at how quickly things can change. Two of our close friends were engaged within four months of getting out of bad relationships. You don't have to immediately join a computer dating service or find a new hobby, but it couldn't hurt. Take advantage of your new free time. Plan a trip somewhere you never thought you'd go, rekindle your friendship with your college roommate. And just when you're starting to get back in the groove again, just when you least expect it, there he'll be. No, not your therapist. Your future husband.

Closing Your Big Fat Multiculti Wedding

10

EVERYONE ON THE PLANET IS CULTURED. Whether you grew up in the hills of North Carolina or the plains of Spain, you are the product of the culture in which you were raised. We decided to bring up the multiculti issue here because that demographic has become a tidal wave that more than one of our readers are going to be riding. We know that if you are in one of these fabulous multicultural relationships, how you handle the cultural land mines will be crucial to how you close the deal.

Just take a look at what happened in *My Big Fat Greek Wedding*, in which a daughter of Greek immigrants falls madly in love with her polar opposite—a Chicago WASP—and it seems that their families will never get along. The movie hit home for a lot of people because, by and large, they identified with the everygirl who maintained her cultural heritage despite *whom* she loved. And of course everyone could relate to the universal and political crises that occur when bringing together two families (even those of the same culture). The public saw themselves in their own movie; whether they inserted into the title Italian, Irish, Jewish, or whatever their ethnic or religious heritage happened to be.

In this chapter we'll introduce you to women who not only closed the deal but have found happiness despite *and because of* their differences. We chose to interview only happily married couples that managed to find solutions and compromises to the countless trials they faced on the way to the altar because they are the ones who will inspire those of you in multicultural relationships. Of course, even if you're not in a mixed-heritage relationship, you'll be inspired by these couples' commitment to each other and how they have made relationships work for the long haul.

The Melting Pot Is a Bottomless Pit

THE GRADUAL BREAKDOWN OF CULTURAL and neighborhood dividing lines seems to be an inevitable and universal experience. These days different ethnicities cohabitate and commingle as never before. Public schools, civil rights, and other factors have created new generations who not only intermingle at an early age but also, for the most part, have learned to accept if not embrace their neighbors' cultural heritage. Your acknowledgment and acceptance of all that is different can greatly affect your decision on who is right for you.

Guess Who's Coming to Dinner, the landmark movie starring Katharine Hepburn, Spencer Tracy, and Sidney Poitier, shows us how an upper-class San Francisco family deals with the issues on the evening they meet their daughter's African-American fiancé and his parents. While *Guess Who's Coming to Dinner* was a watershed movie in 1967, things have changed so dramatically over the past four decades that quite often biracial couples are barely recognized as such. Just look at the episodes of *Sex and the City* in which the white Miranda Hobbes (Cynthia Nixon) was dating the black Dr. Robert Leeds (Blair Underwood). The subject of their different races isn't highlighted on the show and was barely mentioned in the media.

However, as color-blind as the media has become, many real-life families are still sensitive to cultural and religious issues when it affects their sons or daughters. All kinds of questions and concerns can be raised: Will the new person coming into our family accept or reject our culture? Who is going to pass on the family's great rollatini recipe? How are the children going to be raised and in which house of worship—church, synagogue, mosque, or Buddhist temple? These are normal, natural questions that deserve answers.

We've learned a lot from our multiculti conversations about what can be hazardous or helpful to your relationship.

Multiculti's Golden Rule

SINCE NEITHER ONE OF US HAD A MULTICULtural or interfaith marriage, we interviewed a myriad of couples in as many available permutations we could find: young, old, black, white, Asian, Jewish, Catholic, Protestant, Buddhist, and Muslim. Though our research did cover a wide spectrum, we highlight here only those couples that we thought you could learn from: those that had successful relationships by overcoming cultural issues. After all, as our mantra goes, closing the deal is one thing, but keeping it happily closed forever is what we're really after.

In interview after interview, we discovered that the same truth kept surfacing: If you want to marry multiculti, the golden rule is always *compromise*. Compromise? That sounds so simple, doesn't it? And it is . . . until you're the one who has to start compromising. Most likely you'll have to compromise in many aspects of your relationship, but when it takes on a multicultural spin, it often adds up to an entirely different and more difficult scenario. Worse still, some people have little forewarning that a situation where compromise is needed is around the corner. Many couples expressed their love for their partner but also recognized that in the process of closing the deal there were not only land mines but also potential deal breakers to contend with. Here are a couple of "I love you, buts" that you may have to deal with:

But . . . You May Have to Give Up Your Religion

Ruth, who has been happily married to Rocco for fifty-six years, intermarried at a time when it wasn't as culturally accepted.

Rocco, a devout Catholic, who once even considered the priesthood, was very clear with Ruth that not raising their children Catholic would be a marriage deal breaker. A nonobservant Jew, Ruth decided that it was a sacrifice she was willing to make. Ruth's parents, on the other hand, were not thrilled at the prospects of her marrying "out" and of their grandchildren's getting baptized. All the same, Ruth and Rocco's love flourished and their bond grew stronger as they stuck together and faced the difficulties with their parents. Eventually Ruth's parents agreed to attend the baptism party (but not the church service), and Ruth and Rocco were decidedly relieved.

Compromise? Yes. Giving of yourself? Yep. Putting the other person before you? Always. We're not advocating that you compromise yourself or your beliefs, but when differences arise, the first question you must ask is "What do I want?" Interfaith issues can be volatile *and* uncomfortable, and they can often result in the demise of the relationship, so in our opinion you must always discuss faith before closing the deal. (More on this in a bit.)

But . . . You Have to Move to My Country

Man-Ying, a Chinese-born marketing executive, became engaged to Tom, a native New Yorker, while he was working in advertising in Hong Kong. Man-Ying has ten brothers and sisters and is very close with her family. Right around the time Tom proposed, his company wanted to relocate him to their New York office. At that point, Man-Ying and Tom had a big decision to make. Either Tom could look for a new job and stay in Hong Kong or he could continue on the fast track with his company and take the promotion in New York. That would mean that Man-Ying would have to move and leave her family, not to mention getting married in a foreign country without her relatives, as they all could not afford to come over for the celebration that would be later that year.

Tom spoke to his supervisor at work, who offered to create the same position in the San Francisco office, if that would make things easier. Even though Tom really wanted to move back to New York to be near his family, he understood that San Francisco was a closer plane flight for Man-Ying and would relieve much of the pressure on both of them. It was a hard decision, one that is still painful for Man-Ying: She also had to forgo having her parents at her wedding when she moved to the States, and, although she can afford to fly home once a year, it still feels like too little time with her parents as they get older. However, it *was* a compromise, and in the long run well worth it to them both.

While on the outside it may seem that Man-Ying and Ruth "gave up" more than their spouses, they will be the first to tell you that a great relationship is never about the perfect fifty-fifty split. Neither do they think that the compromises they made are worth more than the love they have gained. If neither of you is ready to compromise, don't expect to be doing any kind of deal closing. As you will soon see, the couples we'll introduce you to figured that out for themselves.

Religion: The Patron Saint of All Deal Blowers

RELIGION SHOULD BE A SOURCE OF STRENGTH and foundation for a relationship, not a well of resentment or bitterness. Just because religion might not have played a major role in your life up to now or even in your courting doesn't mean it won't play a role in the near or distant future. Even couples of similar faiths often find that religious counseling helps if one of the partners is more religious than the other.

While the old adage that people of similar faiths have an easier time because the children's religions won't be an issue is probably true, there are still many successful interfaith marriages.

Say "No" to Avoidance!

Religion is such a significant subject that even when there are obvious issues that must be dealt with, couples may delay discussion because they seem too difficult to face. Interfaith marriages are more common than ever, but all the same, discussions regarding ritual and children can generate plenty of discord, so this issue requires careful and early handling. While there is no shortage of interfaith clergy who tag-team at weddings nowadays, it's imperative to have a clear picture of where you're *both* headed after the ceremony.

Even if you try to ignore the issue, at some point it often becomes unavoidable. One of our Catholic friends wanted a church wedding and was faced with the task of getting his Protestant partner-to-be to sign a document before the ceremony that specified that they would bring up their children Catholic. Another couple we know couldn't find a rabbi willing to marry them because the bride's mother wasn't Jewish. If these unresolved issues are left to the last minute, they will yield tense situations, often involving your future in-laws.

How couples plan to fit tradition into their lives together can set families on edge and cause parents to walk down the aisle with hollow eyes and fake, plastered smiles, looking as if they're being led to slaughter. We've seen a few of those. They were weddings to remember, but for all the wrong reasons. You want to have as much figured out as early as possible before you plan one of the most significant parties of your life.

What should you keep in mind as you get closer to closing the multiculti deal? We offer some simple, homespun advice for when complex issues do arise. Extra-special sensitivity needs to be taken on all levels, large and small. For example, respect the feelings and beliefs of elderly or religious relatives who, while they do love you, may be attached to some very strong dogma or doctrine with which you do not agree.

During all these conversations, please keep in mind your 'tude and what you learned in Chapter 5. Take deep breaths and remain calm and rational if the discussions get heated (and they most likely will). You don't want to regret anything.

Have It "Their Way"—the Joining the Club Model

Generally speaking, couples of different faiths very often have varying levels of religious involvement. One successful marriage model is to simply "join the club." According to quite a few of the successful couples we spoke to, the religion issue was most readily solved when the more indifferent spouse complied with the spouse who had the deepest feelings and traditions. Issues like child rearing or conversion are such life-altering issues that there needs to be plenty of discussion and education before walking down the aisle. Know what you're getting into when you decide to "join the club," as once you're in it's hard to get out! Also, not completely solving this early on can create a confusing and disruptive environment, which can create even more problems in the future.

Lyle and Joanna are a loving couple who have everything in common, their religious backgrounds being one of the exceptions. While Joanna isn't extremely religious, she knows that she would be disappointing her parents and grandparents if she married and didn't raise her children Jewish. Lyle is a lapsed Catholic and has no interest in religion but has decided to wed in a Jewish ceremony and raise his children Jewish because he understands that Joanna has deeply rooted feelings about it. He also appreciates the warmth of Joanna's family and since his parents live abroad he knows that he will be spending more time with her family. While Lyle is not converting, he has decided to comply with Joanna and her family and have it "their way."

The Dual Citizenship Model

Can couples of different faiths marry, retain their own individual religions and traditions, and raise their children exposing them to both? Of course they can. There are many successful interfaith couples we spoke to who preferred not to relinquish anything before they took the plunge. Like a seasoned traveler who travels extensively across many borders and time zones, these couples embrace what we call **Dual Citizenship,** living and loving in both states. What makes their unions work is a special brand of interfaith tolerance, compromise, and curiosity. This arrangement is becoming more common, and as children of mixed marriages also marry, the permutations are endless. However, we offer a note of caution: Dual Citizenship has to work *both ways.* Unless a couple is truly committed to sharing in the responsibility equally, resentment can build. If it's truly embraced by both, the results can be ideal.

Our friends Kristin and Keith are a true example of a multifaith mélange. Keith, who was born Jewish, first married an Episcopalian and had two girls who were exposed to both Christianity and Judaism. After divorcing, Keith married Kristin, a Catholic woman with strong beliefs. With a new baby on the way, there was no doubt that flexibility and compromise needed to be part of the equation, as Keith's teenage daughters were living with them every other weekend.

Keith and Kristin embody the Dual Citizenship model. They both attend each other's family events with great respect and interest. Keith explained to us that you really do have to give to get: "To make this work I have to be just as open and interested in attending her church on Christmas as she is in attending my family's Passover seder. If you can't do that, you're really not offering dual citizenships to your spouse and to your kids." If you want your partner to cross borders, you must be willing to embrace their customs as well, not only for your partner, but also for your children. If you're willing and able to do this—to give and take—then maybe having membership in the Dual Citizenship club is right for you. If you think you might end up just paying lip service to this idea, you may end up getting deported.

"Take the Best and Leave the Rest"

While organized religion plays a part in many healthy, happy relationships there are also plenty of couples that create their own custom spirituality instead. Two such couples include our friends, Atoosa Rubenstein, the Muslim-born editor-in-chief of *Seventeen* magazine and her Jewish husband, Ari, and television journalist Judy Licht, who is Jewish while her husband, ad-man extraordinaire Jerry Della Femina, is Catholic.

In both cases, the couples were disenchanted with their respective organized religions and decided to "create their own." They pick and choose the cultural and symbolic aspects of their religions that are important to them, celebrating the cultural traditions of both while instilling their personal ethical beliefs. They select from their own distinctive smorgasbord of cultures and religions to "take the best and leave the rest." Both Atoosa and Judy call their successful model *Rubensteinism* and *Della Feminaism* respectively.

In this model there was an open discussion about both religions; the children were neither encouraged nor discouraged from choosing or participating in either. Emphasis was placed on being a good person and finding a belief and value system that both parents and children find fulfilling. While the children were not regularly exposed early on to organized tradition or religious services, the parents explained to the children the various cultural traditions with less emphasis on the religious rites. For example, Judy explained and educated her children on the importance of the holidays because she felt she needed to "do her job." However, pursuing the religion was totally optional to her children; ultimately, one chose to go to religious school and the other did not.

While "create your own" is the most liberal model we have discussed here, there are issues in this approach that cannot be overlooked. Certainly, both parties must feel the same way in order for it to work or at least have "buy in"—that is, all involved will take part and believe in what they're doing. In this "take the best" model, neither party chooses to "buy" into any specific organized structure. While this model may sound like a good option for people who are disenchanted with their religious background or who are atheists, it must be noted that it would not work with people who are practicing; also, parents, grandparents or close friends may have issues that *neither* party will choose to honor or participate in *their* religious observance. Additionally, blame may be assigned from your spouse's family if they keep wishing that their son or daughter married someone from the "home team" and wondering what the outcome *would* have been. That can create tension unless all sides are as liberal as you are.

In order to make any of these models work, a consensus is required to sustain a happy, lasting union. So if you're a lapsed Catholic who is marrying a lapsed Protestant who wants to celebrate Kwanzaa, put up a menorah and a wreath during the holidays, or nothing at all; it just might work if all parties are open to it. Just don't expect Grandma Rosemary to be as open about it as you are.

All in all, honoring yourself and your diversity is wonderful, just be careful to take your family into consideration and anticipate the fallout your decision may trigger.

LET'S MEET UP with some other women who have had to take risks and make compromises for the men they love and the families they wanted. We figured you'd want this straight from the source, so here are some bits of the conversations we had with our multiculti subjects:

My Big Fat Greek Wedding: Carla and Georgos

CARLA IS A PROPRIETOR OF ONE OF NEW York's leading catering and event planning companies. She has a no-nonsense approach to her personal and business life. Eight years ago Carla married Georgos, and they have two children.

Us: As a woman who married multiculti, what guidelines can you offer women who want to close the deal?

Carla: It should be natural. You shouldn't have to try too hard.

Us: Did you set out to look for a husband?

Carla: Yes, definitely. I knew that I wanted to have a long-lasting relationship. I met the guys I dated mostly through work. As a caterer and event planner, I would not necessarily *go* to the parties as much as *run* them, and because I was constantly in a working social situation, I always had men approaching me. But none of them was the right one.

Us: How did you meet your husband?

Carla: It was a summer-vacation romance that actually turned into marriage. I met him on a beach in Mykonos. He was very handsome.

Us: Was it love at first sight?

Carla: On some level. It was definitely sexual attraction at first sight. He didn't speak much English. We understood each other, though.

Us: Was the language ever a barrier?

Carla: Not really. When you're with someone who doesn't speak much English, you have to use the purest form of language. No slang, no sarcasm. So having the purest form of language built a much stronger base from day one.

Us: How did your relationship progress? Was closing the deal with someone of another culture more difficult?

Carla: It was long distance at first. I think the advantage and disadvantage you get is two different perspectives. I think for me, his being from Greece and so family oriented was really appealing to me. I'm close with my family, but he's *very* old school.

Us: So what happened?

Carla: I was fortunate in that I met him at the beginning of my trip! We spent twelve whole days together.

Us: So your approach was to take it naturally?

Carla: It was a fun romance. I didn't have any expectations. But I have to say, when I got on the plane to go home, I was bawling my eyes out. I *really* liked him.

Us: So here you met this guy, you have a summer romance. How did you keep it going?

Carla: We missed each other terribly, and we both kept up the correspondence for a few months by mail and phone. Then I just came up with the idea that I *had* to see him one more time to see if the feelings were really there. So I thought, "Let's go to the Caribbean." We went to Jamaica, and that sealed the deal. We both knew that it was forever. After Jamaica we started working on his coming to the States. He actually came off the plane in New York with a ring!

Us: What were some of the challenges to closing the Greek deal?

Carla: I think bridging the two cultures was tough. For example, my being so independent was really hard for him at the beginning. The first few weeks he was here he *could not* get over the idea that I would go out alone with my girlfriends. It upset him. His parents, besides going to work, spent every waking moment together.

Us: How did you resolve that conflict?

Carla: I was older. (Most girls in Greece get married younger.) Here I was, American and so independent, so he eventually understood. That part of me wasn't optional. He learned to like the new country ways, and now he goes out quite a bit with his friends . . . perhaps too much!

Us: Sorry, but we have to ask if you had a big fat Greek wedding.

Carla: Yes! It was in Greece, overlooking the ocean. Plates were broken! And I got pelted in the head with candied almonds. It was wild. Of course, the Americans danced only to the American DJ and sat down when the Greek band came on, and the Greeks danced only to the Greek band and sat down when the American DJ came on.

Us: Sounds like culture shock.

Carla: There *were* some crazy things I had to put up with! My maid of honor *had* to be Greek Orthodox. I had no option and didn't meet her till the week of the wedding.

Us: You never met your maid of honor?

Carla: That's right. She had to be the girlfriend or wife of the best man. And she had to help me get ready!

Us: So there were compromises?

Carla: Yes. For example, there's no name for Carla in Greek, so they took a derivative of my middle name, which is Mary, and they called me Marie during the whole ceremony. Since I didn't understand Greek, I had no idea who Marie was! But I didn't grow up in a religious household and liked the idea of a big church wedding.

Us: Do you think you have had to compromise more than other people do in closing the deal because you are from different cultures?

Carla: I compromised the superficial things, but I got more out of the real stuff in the end.

Us: What do you think are the most important aspects of a successful relationship?

Carla: Openness, honesty, humor, communication, complete confidence, and trust.

Us: So what advice would you give to our readers on closing the deal?

Carla: Go to Mykonos!

No matter how minuscule a compromise may seem, it will be significant to your significant other. Be open to experiences, and unless you're 100 percent against them, don't say no. Carla never overreacted to Georgos's family's ways. She understood—as did he, from the beginning—that there would be cultural misunderstandings, so both had to keep an open mind. Carla and Georgos still negotiate and compromise on how to split their vacations between family in the United States and Greece each year.

My Big Fat Black and White Wedding: Alice and Miles

ALICE IS A BRILLIANT AND ELOQUENT EXECutive at a major advertising agency. Originally from Britain, she now lives in New Jersey with her husband, Miles, and their daughter, Mara. Alice and Miles have been happily married for thirteen years and since they closed the deal are even more in love. Alice is Caucasian and Miles is African-American.

Us: When you were growing up, was the idea of marriage important to you?

Alice: No, but I did want to find a life partner. The white wedding dress and the big wedding was never my fantasy.

Us: How did you and Miles meet?

Alice: I met him at the National Film Theatre. He was visiting London with a friend of my friend.

Us: Was it love at first sight?

Alice: I tapped him on the shoulder, and I remember I got this electric shock like something major had happened. Later in the evening we wandered off by the Thames and they were having a fireworks display and one of the firecrackers landed between us.

Us: So sparks were literally flying.

Alice: You could absolutely say that!

Us: What happened next?

Alice: He went back to the United States, and even though he didn't know me very well he would send me something every week: music tapes, little souvenirs from New York, newspaper clippings. I first found it a bit forward, a very American way to behave, not like any of my other relationships, which I guess were more formal and typically British. It made me a little uncomfortable, but it did make me care about him even more. After we'd been corresponding for two months I found out he told my friend that he was going to marry me.

Us: Were you color-blind at this stage, or was race an issue?

Alice: His being American, not black, was the issue for me.

Us: How so?

Alice: Truthfully, the color of his skin seemed to be more of an issue in America than in Britain. When we were in America I felt that people were *looking*. People just seemed shocked when I introduced them to Miles. It just seemed there were far fewer interracial couples in America. It seemed more normal in London.

Us: So how did you finally hook up for good?

Alice: I came to the States for a vacation about three months after we met. At first I thought it would only be a fling, but then through a series of circumstances I was offered a job in New York. I came, got an apartment, but spent only one night there.

Us: Was it obvious from the start?

Alice: Yes, I felt as if I'd known him forever, maybe even in a former life. He also did something amazing. Before I went on my job interview, he called the ad agency where I'd be interviewing, pretended to be a potential client, and got their credentials so I was completely prepped for the interview, which of course went brilliantly, thanks in part to him.

Us: How did you close the deal?

Alice: I had been working here, living with him, for three or four months, and during his bar exam he was under a great deal of pressure, which is understandable, but I had this feeling that he was starting to lose interest. So I decided to be up front and basically said, "If you're not interested, let me know and I'll move on." I could have moved out that night; I still had my apartment.

Us: Smart girl!

Alice: I always believe a girl should keep her options open.

Us: What did he say?

Alice: He was upset and apologized. He told me he was under a lot of stress, which I knew, but I wanted the relationship to progress, and it did two months later.

Us: Were there any issues in closing the interracial deal?

Alice: To be honest, yes. *We* didn't have any issues with it, but both our families did. My father always said, "Whatever you do, don't marry an American," and I brought home a black American! I don't think they ever expected a black man. Miles's parents also had issues with his being with a white woman.

Us: Was it difficult?

Alice: Extremely. My mother had a breakdown on the telephone when I broke the news. She was scared of what my father would say and started having palpitations. She went to the doctor, who asked her what was wrong, and he said, get this, "I can treat many things, but *racism* isn't something I have medication for"! When she got home she was so worked up, she just told my father, "If you don't like it, I'm moving out." There was a lot of high drama.

Us: And your dad?

Alice: He didn't say much to me. He just went out and, in the British tradition, got drunk. In the end both my parents said, "If you're in love with him, I'm sure he's marvelous." They had faith in the fact that if I loved someone he had to be right for me. They had their one moment of major drama, but that was it.

Us: And his parents?

Alice: They had basically the same reaction.

Us: What are your religious affiliations?

Alice: I'm Catholic, he's Episcopalian.

Us: How are you raising Mara?

Alice: As a Catholic, because I care more about it than Miles. My theory is, if it's something you believe in, raise your child in a religion.

Us: How is your family now?

Alice: They love Miles and think he's fabulous!

Us: And his family?

Alice: Pretty happy. I get along with his parents, but while they're still supportive, I do believe they wish he'd married a black woman, though our families get along very nicely.

Us: Any advice for our readers?

Alice: People in this situation must realize that they're not necessarily making an easy choice. Race is difficult for some people to overcome and may cause pain to the people you love. That was the hardest part for me, knowing that even if my parents were supportive, initially I was causing them pain. It's a heavy burden. So is knowing that when it would come to having children there would be extra issues to deal with. So you do question if the person is right for you. But because there was a certain amount of adversity, we took our love and relationship more seriously. In the end, it does make you stronger, more resilient.

Us: Tell us about your daughter and how she's treated by both sides of the family.

Alice: Mara is five. She is loved and adored by all her grandparents. She does talk a lot about how she's "in between" in color, and we take a lot of time telling her how beautiful she is. She views it as very special, as do we. She's learning early on to embrace the cultural differences.

Us: Tell us what you have learned along the way.

Alice: So much. Some women have criteria in their head

like "What does he do?" "How tall is he?" "How much does he earn?" I think you need to be open to whatever's possible. If you go in with criteria, you limit your options. Look for a person first, not a résumé. I have a motto that I can share: "Be great on your own, but better together." Be yourself. It's problematic when people look for themselves in other people.

Us: Any last thoughts?

Alice: Women are so much more independent today. Don't close the deal for the sake of closing the deal. Close it only if it's a great deal for you!

Though it all worked out for Alice and Miles, it's not always going to be easy. You have to acknowledge your differences, and that people, including your own family, might not see the situation as you do. It may be uncomfortable to discuss the realities of the world, especially when it comes to your love, and it may be difficult to acknowledge that people you love may not be supportive of your choice. In all, this will make you realize—or see clearer—what is better for *you* to do. Just remember what we taught you about managing your 'tude when dealing with family.

My Big Fat Jewish Wedding

KARIN IS A STUNNING AND CEREBRAL BELgian, blond artist who recently closed the deal. Before marrying her long-term, live-in boyfriend Alan, Karin underwent an Orthodox Jewish conversion. (Within the Jewish community, the religious affiliations range from reform, the least observant; to conservative, observant; to Orthodox, the most observant.)

Us: You come from a European background, specifically from Belgium?

Karin: Yes, my background is especially Belgian, very proper. There's a lot of emphasis on how you sit, what you say, and how you say it.

Us: How did you meet Alan?

Karin: I moved to New Jersey with my mother and sister when I was twenty and was going to the Fashion Institute of Technology and taking care of my young sister while my mother worked. I was always a total introvert and happy with my solitude. I really did *not* go out. I was busy with school and was really the last person looking for a boyfriend.

Us: And . . .

Karin: Alan's friend was going out with my friend, and when the friend met me he thought Alan would like me. But at the time I wouldn't agree to a double date. So in an effort to convince me, Alan sent me a letter with his picture.

Us: So you went out with him?

Karin: No. I thought it was nice and he was handsome, but I was too shy. One day a friend said, "Why don't you throw that picture away—you'll never call." So I called. I don't like being told what to do. Alan picked up the phone and said, "I've been waiting."

Us: What did you think of Alan's being Jewish?

Karin: Being Jewish was never a foreign thing to me. Growing up in Belgium, many of my mother's friends were Jewish. For some reason I was always attracted to Jewish people, their wit and charm.

Us: Were there any issues in his family about your not being Jewish?

Karin: Yes. Alan has a very distinct Jewish history. His father was a Holocaust survivor who had been through Auschwitz. Alan was raised in the mind-set of "We're Jews and we're survivors."

Us: And how did he react toward Alan's dating you?

Karin: His father didn't want Alan dating me. It wouldn't have made a difference to him if I converted.

Us: Were you angry?

Karin: No. That's the way he felt. This was an extreme case. His father's family was all killed before his eyes in Auschwitz. I don't have anything against him. I have no animosity toward him. The poor man was tortured! I cannot *imagine* ever being in his shoes.

Us: How did your family react to Alan's father's issues?

Karin: My mother was sad for me. She would say, "How dare they not accept you." We react differently emotionally.

Us: So you couldn't close the deal or get married in the traditional sense?

Karin: No, not unless it was hidden, like an elopement or something. I said no, that wasn't necessary. I thought that if we're together and we have each other and we have each other's hearts, there's no reason for the paper. I didn't need to get married. I also didn't want Alan to be estranged from his family. After all, he was working for his father, who threatened to fire him or disown him if we got married.

Us: How did Alan respond?

Karin: He said, "Go ahead and fire me." At one point he told his dad that he was willing to give up every-thing for me. That's when his father realized how much Alan loved me. Deep down he didn't want Alan not to be a part of the family or to work at the company. He had worked his way up from nothing, and it was all for Alan and his brother, for his children.

Us: When did you decide to convert?

Karin: I decided to convert after his father died. I didn't at first because I felt very uncomfortable, as if I was going to be judged. I had a big fear that I was going to be made to feel as though I didn't belong. I'd felt a lot of that just from being from Belgium and not speaking English at first in the United States. I didn't want more of that. So I put it off.

Us: Do you think it was a deal blower?

Karin: Even if I chose not to convert, I would always want my children to be Jewish, for Alan and for his father. Alan owed his father everything, after all. And I love Alan for who he is. I'm part of Alan now. After all these years, we are *one*. I wanted to do it for his children. Our children.

Us: What did your mother say?

Karin: My mother said she was very proud of me.

Us: What is the recipe for a successful multiculti relationship?

Karin: The recipe for success, in my opinion, is for two people to accept each other's differences, whatever they may be, and never put them down. One must also educate oneself. Don't get completely involved until you know it's what you want. Hold back your heart a bit. For example, you have to visit his family and make sure it's something you can live with despite the difficulties. Only you know if you can deal with it. I believe you shouldn't openly dislike your partner's family. We all tend to sometimes think the person we're with is *only* ours, but there's family involved, and the number-one mistake is to talk negatively. It only puts your partner in the middle. As an example, if I had said to Alan about his father, "This is not right—he's discriminating against me the way he was discriminated against," it would have made matters *worse*. I would *never* want Alan to hate his father. Don't torture him with it, because eventually everything bounces back to you.

Us: Any other advice?

Karin: Make your man feel like a hero every day.

Us: What would you say to the feminists out there?

Karin: We are still different. Men and women are different and not equal. But who said equal is good? How can he be equal to me? I can give birth. I think the act of loving, giving birth, being a mother, is beautiful and glamorous, and I'm proud of it. One day I'll be a mother—a Jewish mother!

Karin's story teaches a lot about marriages of any kind. No matter your religion, race, or culture, you'll have to deal with family, and sometimes it won't be pretty. As we've said before, always remember your 'tude: You don't have to give up your beliefs, just remember that other people are involved.

Now That You Have This Information, How Can You Make It Work for You?

ACCORDING TO OUR EXPERTS, AS IN ANY relationship, the three pillars of closing the multiculti deal are the abilities to accept, forgive, and compromise. Multiculti relationships are like any other relationships, except that they involve a little more work. Just ask yourself: Am I ready to do some heavy lifting? Is my partner ready too?

If you're the type of person who wants a Burger King relationship (you know, to "Have It Your Way"), you might want to reconsider getting yourself into a relationship that will demand more than you're willing to give. If, when you meet someone, you want to change the parts you can't accept and spend countless hours and energy trying to get him to be something he's not, or if you're not ready to face those tough issues, then you're not ready for a multiculti deal-closing ceremony or the long-term commitment that comes afterward.

Don't think sensitive family, cultural, or religious issues are going to work themselves out on their own. Instead of sweeping them under the carpet, do a thorough housecleaning of all the hotbed issues before you accept a ring.

We're pro-compromise, not pro-crastinate. Addressing potential problems and starting sooner rather than later is a good habit to get into and will serve many aspects of your relationship well. So whether you're starring in your own Big Fat Greek, Italian, Armenian, Polish or Hindu Wedding . . . get comprising, and then get closing.

II Successful Women: Successful Deal Closers

TODAY'S SUCCESSFUL DEAL CLOSER ISN'T, perhaps, what you think. She's *not* necessarily the little woman who cares *only* about marriage and family. She can be a smart, sexy, successful postfeminist who knows what she wants and how to get it. She applies the same extremely high standards to her professional life as she applies to her personal one, and she doesn't play games. She wants and gets the balance she seeks, as she won't *settle* for *settling*. *She* could be *you*—or will be soon.

So who are these women and what can we learn from them? We interviewed a broad range of women and asked them to share what they thought had helped them close the deal.

The Shrink's Advice

"Take stock of who you are."
—Patty Stegman

Patricia Stegman, L.C.S.W., holds a degree from Columbia University and did her postgraduate work at the Ackerman Institute for the Family, one of the most renowned marriage and family therapy institutes in the world. She met her husband, Danny, when she was in her late twenties studying at the Stanley Kaplan Test Preparation Center. She currently has a private practice counseling couples and families.

Us: Were you a woman who set out to close the deal?

Patricia: Yes, if that means that I wanted a long-term, fantastic, fulfilling relationship. Something much more than companionship.

Us: So, in the courting phase, how did you handle yourself, or, simply, how do shrinks handle their personal relationships?

Patricia: First and foremost, I took a personal inventory of myself in the dating process. Who was I? What was important? What mattered most to me? I wanted a person who was kind, considerate, intelligent, and warm, and who had good values. And he had to be ambitious. And I shouldn't leave out sexy, romantic, engaging, and honest!

Us: Don't you think that's an awfully long list?

Patricia: No, I think that's a short list and it changes over time.

Us: What was your dating philosophy when you were looking for Mr. Right?

Patricia: To get to know this person as well as I possibly could. And to have lots of fun.

Us: Was it love at first sight with Danny?

Patricia: For me, no.

Us: For him?

Patricia: Yes.

Us: How long did you date before you realized you wanted to marry him?

Patricia: Three months. I saw the way he interacted with my family and I appreciated his character and strengths.

Us: So what guidelines would you offer both professionally and personally to women in this phase of their relationship?

Patricia: I feel a lot of women are not clear on who they are or what's important to them. I often see them jump into a pool without seeing if there's any water in it. Take stock of who you are and who your wannabe partner is before you try to close the deal. Once you have a well-defined sense of who you are, look for someone who complements the assets or deficits that you possess. Ask a lot of questions of the person you are seeing, though not on the first date. For example, "Tell me three things you like most about yourself and three things you would like to change about yourself." Small things are often indicative of larger issues.

And be watchful. If family is important to you, watch how he is with your family. If the environment is important to you, watch how he treats the earth. Do not ignore things that are disturbing. Don't look away. Address issues as they arise.

Us: As a shrink, what do you think the ingredients are for a successful relationship?

Patricia: A professional hero of mine, John Gottman, is one of the very few psychologists who has done research on what makes a good relationship. His findings conclude that one of the keys to a successful relationship is the couple's ability to resolve conflict.

Us: Meaning?

Patricia: Conflict is inevitable. It's how you resolve conflict and move through difficult issues together that will determine how successful your relationship is. I see this with my patients.

Us: What advice would you give to women who wanted to close the deal but didn't know how?

Patricia: Be very clear about what's motivating you to close the deal. The first things I would ask would be "Why do you want to close the deal? What are you hoping for and what are your fantasies?" If you know what's getting in the way of it closing—for example, he says, "I'm afraid to close the deal because of intimacy"—will [the intimacy issue] go away once the deal is closed, or will he still be distant? These things are meaningful.

Us: You obviously treat many female and male patients in their relationships. What's the difference between those patients who have successful relationships and those who are unsuccessful?

Patricia: The unsuccessful ones try to just fill a void like loneliness, or [they get married] because they think it's what they *have* to do, as opposed to a good relationship, where the participants are very clear about who they are. They also see very, *very clearly* who the other person is.

Us: Thanks, Shrink Patty!

What We Hope You Take with You Know yourself. Shrink Patty has an excellent sense of self—and great self-confidence—and this translated into her knowing what she wanted in a life partner. Not only do you want to know your partner and have an undistorted view of him, but in order to do that, you need to be clear with yourself. Remember, you're *not* closing the deal just for the sake of it—you're closing it for that lasting bond. Know if he's the one only by knowing *you*.

Being Super Woman!

"Marriage is a partnership,
but you'd better treat it more like a business."
—Marisa Acocella Marchetto

Marisa Acocella Marchetto is a leading cartoonist for *The New Yorker* and the author of *She,* an illustrated novel. Marisa is celebrated for her stylish depictions of women and their urban angst (as seen in this book) and has had one-woman shows sponsored by Chanel and Ferragamo. After several years together, Marisa and Silvano Marchetto, the celebrated Florentine restaurateur, recently got married!

Us: What do you think of what you've read in *Closing the Deal?*

Marisa: I think it's genius, not just because you're one of my best friends, and I'm doing the cartoons for the book, but because I have always asked you boyfriend advice (for the past twenty years).

Us: So, Marisa, how did you go about closing the deal with New York's premier restaurateur, the famous Silvano of Da Silvano?

Marisa: Basically, it's like cooking. Your book is a great recipe, but you need true love to make the wedding cake.

Us: You flatter us.

Marisa: You're right, but your advice is helpful to women, because women don't understand guys the way guys understand guys!

Us: So how did you work your magic on one of New York's most desired guys?

Marisa: I was just a normal person and not like every other gal throwing herself at an eligible guy.

Us: Meaning, you didn't give it up on the first date.

Marisa: I knew him for twenty years; we had a friendship from the restaurant. I also had my own life, and my own career. I wasn't expecting him to "rescue" me.

Us: Did your Italian connection have anything to do with it?

Marisa: Yes, we did have a lot in common, which is a good thing.

Us: Silvano is older than you, with a grown daughter in her twenties.

Marisa: That was never an issue. I don't judge age, just the character. And his daughter is such a great girl and we have a great relationship. I always wanted a daughter but never wanted to give birth.

Us: So, Marisa, did the advice we gave you (that we put in our book) really help you?

Marisa: Yes, and it'll be helpful to *all* women.

Us: How? Give it up.

Marisa: With pleasure. One main message that I took was that marriage is a partnership, but you'd better treat it like it's a business or your livelihood. Operate on a business timetable, as opposed to a "relationship" timetable. For example, if [your boyfriend] needs something, do it right then and there, so you don't lose your most important account. Many women have become great at business, but a lot of women suck at their personal relationships. They're so focused on being successful at work, they forget to try to be successful at home. After all, telling a woman today that she's a good wife is a put-down in some circles. I believe part of being successful is *also* having a successful marriage.

Us: Any other advice for our girls out there?

Marisa: Men are not stupid. They see through the attempts to manipulate, and if you're real and what you do comes from the heart, then you won't have to invest as much in plastic surgery.

Us: What advice in this book did you follow that helped you close the deal?

Marisa: The Scheherazade Factor. I always had something to say, but I was never overt about it.

Us: How do you two resolve your conflicts?

Marisa: We talk it out. Having a sense of humor or laughing your way out of a problem is always the best way to resolve a conflict.

Us: Favorite chapter?

Marisa: "The Art of the Bluff."

Us: Why?

Marisa: Because you're dealing from a position of strength. The concept made me think of how much I gave of myself before I got the ring. It's important for people to realize how valuable they are.

Us: Any last thoughts?

Marisa: Don't become the woman who gives so much away that you also give away your [self-]respect.

What We Hope You Take with You

Marisa readily admits that she is a woman born to a conflicted generation, whose mothers gave up careers for daughters who in turn made careers their top priority. But many women like Marisa who have achieved professional success also want the other half of the equation. We love Marisa's point about the importance of putting as much effort into your relationship as into your work, and its coming from a successful deal closer makes it even better—especially because we couldn't agree more. Don't take yourself for granted. (And don't take your man for granted either.)

The Happy Ending

"A successful relationship is about shared goals."
—Adriana Trigiani

When Adriana Trigiani wrote *Big Stone Gap,* she didn't realize that it would touch the hearts of Americans. Subsequently, that novel and the ones that followed, including *Lucia, Lucia* and *The Queen of the Big Time* have all been *New York Times* bestsellers. Adriana is known for her sense of humor, her love of family, her welcoming nature, and her amazing lasagna. Did life just happen to Adri, or did she write her own happy outcome? Let's see.

Us: How did you close the deal?

Adri: We met in 1988 at Lehigh University but didn't get together until two years later. Tim was the technical director for my one-act play *True Colors*. He says he fell in love with me when I walked into the theater one day wearing jeans and a William "Refrigerator" Perry football jersey. That's a hint to my sisters out there: I was in jeans, not Manolo Blahniks. Tim says a man knows when he's hooked, though he might not admit it right away. I really closed the deal on our first date. Tim had been ambivalent about getting involved with me for a variety of reasons, so when he came to his senses, I told him that he had to commit then and there. Of course he did, but then I proceeded to run from the altar. Four years later I finally came to *my* senses, and we've been happily married for eight years.

Us: What was your philosophy on dating?

Adri: I questioned myself a lot. I thought, "What is wrong with me, why can't I get this party started?" I thought and think now, I was so driven to succeed at my work that I didn't have *time* for men. And, of course, I fell in love with several gay men, which is always the mark of an artist.

Us: What was the most important thing you looked for in a man?

Adri: I looked for character. Decency. A big heart. I found it.

Us: What do you think the aspects of a successful relationship are?

Adri: A successful relationship is about shared goals. A man has to take your dreams seriously. You have to take *his* seriously. And the home has to be a *home*, full of love, good food, and comfort. Your husband should *race* home to you. And you should *race* home to him.

Us: Did being a successful writer pose any challenges to closing the deal?

Adri: I was lucky. There were no challenges. My success has only enhanced our lives. My husband is in awe of me and I of him. We know that people are happy when they are productive and creative, so we give each other a lot of support in the work arena.

Us: What advice would you give women who want to close the deal but don't know how?

Adri: A woman needs to have personal clarity to attract what she wants, whether it's at the office or in her heart. You should be honest with the guy you're seeing. Tell him how you feel. After college, Tim came out to visit me in California, where I was writing for the show *A Different World*. When he got off the plane I asked him what his intentions were. I told him I'd be happy to just be friends. That was a lie, but I convinced myself that friendship would have been enough. But that dialogue got the ball rolling. After you tell him how you feel, listen to what he says and *believe* him. If he doesn't want to get married and you do, get out of it. Honor your intuition and use your strength. Being married is just one way of living. It isn't for everyone. But if you want it, you should be able to have it. So stick to your guns.

Us: What guidelines can you offer women from your viewpoint?

Adri: Be yourself. Lead an interesting, fascinating life for *you*, and the rest will follow.

What We Hope You Take with You   While Adri was one of those women who knew what they wanted from the beginning, we're sure it was easier for her because she had a clear vision of who she was—that's what we love about her. Also, we know that being clear and laying your intentions on the line (when the timing is right) are crucial to deal closing and having a real and solid relationship. And Adri's creation of a warm and comfortable home is also greatly appealing to many men.

Ninety-Six Years Old and Still Kicking Up Her Heels

> *"If your husband ever asks for sex,*
> *never have a bellyache or a headache."*
> —Shirley Travis

Shirley Travis has a lot to say. At ninety-six, with an active career on the stage (she recently starred in *Hello, Dolly!* at the Fountainbleau in Miami) and a full-time boyfriend, who wouldn't? Shirley has done it all, from winning beauty contests at fifteen to appearing as a showgirl in the Ziegfeld Follies to marrying in her early twenties and having four children, eight grandchildren, and eight great-grandchildren. Shirley reignited her career when she won the Glamorous Grandmother contest of 1955. She's been back in rhinestones and feathers ever since, and we thought she could teach us about closing the deal, '20s-style.

Us: How did you become a Ziegfeld girl?

Shirley: When I was fifteen I snuck out of school in Brooklyn and entered the Miss Bensonhurst Beauty Contest. I won the Loving Cup Award, was discovered, and ended up working for Ziegfeld, the Shuberts, and the rest of 'em.

Us: Did your parents know?

Shirley: They were horrified. My mother said, "Over my dead body." In those days if you were a chorus girl it was a disgrace, especially if you were a nice Jewish girl like me!

Us: How did you meet your husband?

Shirley: He was in the audience.

Us: A stage door Johnny?

Shirley: Nah! He was in dental school. He was older and very successful!

Us: So you closed the deal, just like that?

Shirley: No. I really loved him but his parents didn't want to him to marry me. I was a chorus girl and he was becoming a dentist, a doctor.

Us: How did you get him to close the deal? What happened?

Shirley: I was on the road while he was in school and he sent me letters. Eventually I said to him, "Irwin, are you going to listen to your parents for the rest of your life or what?" I *never* thought he was going to marry me! Finally after two years, I made it clear. I said, "Don't you think it's about time?" But in those days you didn't get engaged without a ring. And he had no money, so I asked my mother, who had a lot of jewelry, to give me one of her rings. I asked Irwin if he would accept it. He said he would. It was a two-carat diamond. Very nice.

Us: So your mother was in on the act?

Shirley: Of course. She also threw the engagement party, and we set the date for January.

Us: And that's when you got married?

Shirley: No way. I wasn't stupid. His parents were pressuring him to break up with me, and I didn't want him to back out. I got nervous, so I asked him to meet me at City Hall. No one ever knew except my mother. We were married in June of 1929 and went through with the religious ceremony in January 1930, and his parents never knew! It's so interesting. By the time we actually had the big wedding in January it was 1930, the Depression, and my parents had gone bankrupt. Irwin paid for everything, the wedding, the new house, the furniture—he even paid for my parents to move. He was such a decent man.

Us: What was the relationship like with his parents once you were married?

Shirley: Polite. I was very nice, but I had all these little heartaches knowing that they didn't want him to marry me. I was bothered by it, but they never, ever knew. I never said anything.

Us: Why not?

Shirley: What's the point? What's the benefit of saying something bad about your husband's parents?

Us: What was your attitude toward sex in marriage?

Shirley: My mother said, "Shirley, don't ever say no. If your husband ever asks for sex, never have a bellyache or a headache."

Us: Do you agree with your mother's advice?

Shirley: Yes, I certainly do. I think that's why a lot of men cheat—their wives won't do it. I have a lot of friends who after having children told me, "I'm closing up shop"—in every sense! And they were very nice ladies, all married to doctors. They just closed up shop.

Us: Was that the secret to your happy marriage?

Shirley: Part of it is that I really catered to him. I did everything for him. I'm not lying when I tell you we had a wonderful relationship. We were very, very happy together. Fifty-seven years! And I'm not just saying that in my old age. I really loved him. We never ever raised our voices. We never said bad things to each other. Well, we did have one fight in 1930, but he told me, "Shirley, you must never speak to me like that and I will never speak to you like that. We have to have mutual respect." And we did.

Us: Shirley, what do you think is the number-one ingredient for a successful marriage?

Shirley: Compassion. What you give is what you get.

Us: Now for the good stuff. Tell us about your current boyfriend.

Shirley: Ben is ninety-two. My grandson, who's a doctor, was treating him for his prostate and said, "You have to meet my grandmother. You won't be disappointed."

Us: So, you still went out on a blind date at ninety-four?

Shirley: Sure, why not? He was so excited, he left his keys in the car and the motor running.

Us: Are you active?

Shirley: If you mean sexually, say it.

Us: Do you have a lot of sex?

Shirley: You wouldn't believe it, and I'm not lying. He gets me very excited. He's younger than me, and he is a very passionate man.

Us: Do you want to get married again?

Shirley: No way! I like my independence. We have sex here, but he doesn't sleep over. Other women want to get married—they try to grab them, live with them. I won't do that. I won't live with him and I won't give up my friends.

Us: Does your boyfriend treat you nicely?

Shirley: Nice is an understatement. You should see the cruises, the jewelry he buys me! Not that I don't have my own . . . the jewelry my husband gave me is priceless.

Us: Shirley, you're a true Ziegfeld Girl, through and through.

Shirley: That's right, doll!

What We Hope You Take with You Shirley is a great example of a woman who never let age define or inhibit her. She has remained beautiful not only because of her great looks but because she has and always had a positive attitude. The way she tells it: "Everywhere I go, people cannot believe I'm ninety-six. They think I'm in my sixties, seventies. I think it's because I'm a very positive person. I've always been very happy-go-lucky. I don't look for problems and they don't look for me. I don't complain."

Shirley's relationships have benefited from her savvy and smarts, combined with determination and an optimistic spirit to succeed. The fact that she never talked badly about her in-laws who never fully accepted her is a testament to positive thinking and behavior. And, of course, we love what she has to say about sex. While we're not saying a lack of sex is definitely the cause for the breaking up of marriages—that's a "chicken or egg" discussion—we can't help wondering whether a good dose of Shirley's attitude toward sex would get more marriages lasting fifty-plus years!

The American Dream

"I think it's really important to dream big dreams
and to hold on to them."
—Phyllis George

Phyllis George is both a pioneer and an American icon. The most famous Miss America and the first female television sportscaster, Phyllis, at fifty-five, is as beautiful today as when she won her crown in 1971. Her life reads like a romance novel. First married to the legendary producer Robert Evans *(Love Story, The Godfather)* and then to the former governor John Y. Brown Jr., Phyllis has a skin-care line called "Phyllis George Beauty" that debuted on the Home Shopping Network in October 2004 and is the author of the inspirational bestseller *Never Say Never*. Phyllis is now a single mother of two and lives in New York. Phyllis let us take a peek into the private life of a very public person. And although she's currently single, there is a lot we can learn from a double deal closer.

Us: You've been married twice, correct?
Phyllis: Yes. My first marriage was to the Hollywood producer Robert Evans. I was twenty-seven. What can I say—we were married for five minutes.

Us: Five minutes?

Phyllis: Well, I married him after a serious five-year relationship with someone else had ended; it really only lasted eight months. [My marriage to Bob] helped me realize what I truly wanted and what I didn't want. Bob didn't want kids, the big Southern house, church on Sundays, or the whole white picket fence thing, and *I* didn't want life in the fast lane.

Us: And you didn't know that before the wedding?

Phyllis: What did I know? Even though I was Miss America, I was a fresh-faced kid from Denton, Texas, with small-town values. He introduced me to a life I never knew. He was an utter gentleman, had impeccable taste, and oh, that house! The most gorgeous house in Beverly Hills . . .

Us: And you didn't get to keep the house?

Phyllis: That's the whole point. It was *his* house. It would never have been my house or even *our* house . . .

Us: So, you folded?

Phyllis: Precisely. The deal wasn't right.

Us: Do you regret it?

Phyllis: No. I was exposed to Hollywood at its best. It was a fantasy, a dream, but it wasn't my dream.

Us: And husband number two, John Y. Brown, former governor of Kentucky?

Phyllis: Well, he wasn't governor when I first met him. He was one of the original founders of Kentucky Fried Chicken (now KFC) before we were married.

Us: Now, how did you close the deal with John Y.?

Phyllis: Actually, I must say, he set his sights on me. In fact, during my brief first marriage he even bought the house next to Evans's in Beverly Hills. I'd actually met John much earlier. It was a question of timing. He always said he wanted to "take Phyllis Ann back to Kentucky."

Us: And you let him?

Phyllis: Not before he took me to Aspen! We fell in love in Aspen.

Us: Are you revealing that you actually went away with him? In *that* sense?

Phyllis: John and I were dating seriously at that point and, yes, I did take a risk and go away with him. Sometimes you need to do that, take a leap of faith and jump, but it was a *real* relationship and the timing was right. I can honestly say it was the most wonderful time of my life. We had such great chemistry for each other. When we came off our honeymoon to the campaign trail, they used to call it the "kissing campaign" because we couldn't keep our hands off each other.

Us: So you're a big believer in chemistry?

Phyllis: Chemistry and compromise. Once the chemistry is there and you know it's a deal you want to close, everyone has to give a little, take a little. Don't break up the game.

Us: Now, some of our readers might be saying, "Well, I'm not a former Miss America." What advice do you have for our readers out there?

Phyllis: First of all, you have to determine if it's a deal you want to close. Is there chemistry? Do you come from different or similar backgrounds, and how does that affect your relationship? Do you have similar values? One should ask whether she sees it as a deal for the long term, as marriage is all about the long term. If you have tried and it doesn't work, get out. My friend Kenny Rogers had a song that went, "Know when to hold 'em, know when to fold 'em." Certainly, you have to know who you're with. Men don't change, and, for the most part, women don't change either.

Us: So . . . does Miss America give it up on the first date?

Phyllis: Absolutely not! I'm very old school on this issue. When I won Miss America, I can tell you, I was a virgin. I was scared to death. I still believe that you should experience intimacy with someone you're emotionally involved with. I don't care what you say: It's hard to detach your feelings, no matter what the current mores are. And I can tell you, few men want a woman who's been passed around. I've heard it when I was working in the sports world, doing interviews as a sports-caster, and I always told my daughter, you should wait and save yourself for your Prince Charming. It's what every mother wants for her daughter.

Us: What would you say is the one thing a woman should do to close the deal?

Phyllis: Make sure you have your own life in order. Don't give up your own identity. Learn to be alone and be able to take care of yourself. If you can be alone, you're ready for a real relationship. Have confidence, but don't try to close the deal on a bad day. If you're too persistent or jealous, he'll run. Play it cool.

Us: Any other inside tips from the runway?

Phyllis: Men love to talk about themselves. Ask loads of questions about them and listen. It never fails.

Us: Do you think age is a factor in closing the deal?

Phyllis: Absolutely not! I know so many girls in their

twenties who are not dating. I'm fifty-five, and today I feel younger and more confident because of all my experiences. I may have messed up, but I've always bounced back. I honestly think a lot of it starts with a positive attitude. If you are happy and surround yourself with positive people, it can make you look ten years younger, and you are fun to be around. Beauty comes from within, and I know this sounds crazy, but good hygiene is important. My mother always said, "Pretty is as pretty does." Looks fade away, but personality is forever. Guess who was Miss Congeniality?

Us: Any last Southern secrets?

Phyllis: First of all, I believe everyone has something special about her or him. But I will say, "Follow your dreams." There is no question that Miss America catapulted me into the big leagues. But even though I was from a small town in Texas, I always knew I would end up in a big city like New York anyway. There were an awful lot of Miss Americas who chose to stay in their hometowns and marry their childhood sweethearts, which of course isn't a bad thing. But I was different. I always, always dreamed. I think it's really important to dream big dreams and hold on to them, and then turn your dreams into reality. But always remember, girls, if you want to close the deal, don't forget your lip gloss.

What We Hope You Take with You Exterior beauty is always appealing to a man, but not every woman has Phyllis's positive outlook, and we're sure that's what attracts the men—and keeps them coming. Confidence, self-esteem, and good manners are timeless assets for many men. Phyllis's sense of tradition may seem a bit old school for some young women today, but her values are time-honored and it's logic that would put any young woman in good stead. We see from her experiences that the more a woman knows who she is and what she wants, the better her relationship could be. We do think that Phyllis's outlook on getting out of a relationship that isn't working is both honest and modern.

What You *Must* Take with You

THE GENERAL THREAD THROUGH ALL THESE interviews is that when a woman has a sense of self and knows what she wants, the better the relationship. Men love independent, confident, compassionate women with positive energy. To quote one woman we love, "If you want to close the deal, get a life."

Even if you aren't a career gal or don't intend to be, while you're in a relationship it's still important to maintain your own interests, hobbies, groups of friends, and your sense of self. You'll be happier for it.

Another interesting and common thread among these fabulous ladies was that they were actively participating in their partnerships. No matter how successful these women are, they are "givers" and not "takers." Each woman is nurturing in her own unique way, and that's an essential part of deal closing. Many of the single women we talked to had a sense of entitlement, which is not exactly a turn-on. Not every successful woman is a successful deal closer, but many deal closers we met were successful at whatever it was they held *most* dear.

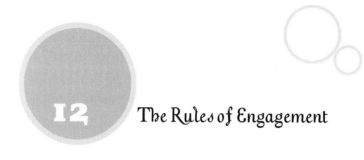

The Rules of Engagement

CONGRATULATIONS, YOU'VE EARNED THE right to read this chapter. Hopefully your ring is exactly what you've always dreamed of. And if this book did its job, your man is too. If that's the case, take pride in your accomplishment.

Now is the time to celebrate and enjoy your new status as couple du jour! However, because we've tried to be honest with you the whole way through, we're going to tell you that now is *not* the time to become overconfident. Although you may think so, you're not on dry land yet. Yes, you may have a gold and diamond life preserver, but you haven't made it all the way to the happily-ever-after coastline.

With that in mind, we offer some words of advice, culled from years of groomsmen events and, more important (for this chapter), "I just got divorced" men's dinners! We've heard *all* the stories, stories of the couples who for years and years were a wonderful fit but headed for Splitsville soon after becoming engaged. What went wrong? Perhaps it had something to do with a family's meddling nature, previously bottled up like champagne, that finally uncorked in a frothy explosion right after the engagement. Or perhaps it was the awesome fear of a life of monogamy that drove one of the parties to drink. By compiling a list of potential scenarios, we, with any luck, will be able to prevent some major last-minute deal blowing.

The Mind of the Engaged Man

WHAT HAPPENED TO YOUR MAN IN THE weeks leading up to the Big Question? The engagement period works differently for men and women. What if we told you that, though it *should* be a wonderful time for both of you, it could be a much better time for only one of you and a difficult, transitory time for the other. Finding it hard to imagine your man having a more wonderful time than you? It can happen. In fact, it happened to one of us. Let us take you inside the head of a guy who's just proposed, so you know what you'll be dealing with.

Preengagement, some men go through what we call **Engagement Purgatory**, during which they will weigh their decision very carefully. A man may exhibit signs of stress, causing him to appear somewhat moody, perhaps even distant or distracted. In this emotional period, there are conflicting voices battling it out in his head. For example:

Voice one: "I'm going to be with the girl of my dreams for the rest of my life!"

Voice two: "I'm going to be sleeping with only the girl of my dreams for the rest of my life!"

The decision to propose is a huge leap for most men. He may be trying to comprehend never going out on another date; basically, never again having the level of independence he enjoyed as a bachelor. (Like we mention at the start of the book, this change is comparable, in our opinion, to giving birth for women—so, obviously, a bit of stress is involved.) But if you've gotten to this point, then you've followed our advice successfully, so feel confident that you'll be able to maneuver through this purgatory.

Once he's over these hurdles and he's asked and you've accepted the proposal, what may occur next is a period we call **Engagement Euphoria.** Most men, having made that final decision to commit, feel a tremendous sense of relief, resulting in an overwhelming expression of excitement. You may now hear him say things like "Wow, being engaged is so great. Had I known, I would have done it sooner!" Or the ever popular "I wish we could be engaged forever."

Most likely, this will result in friends, coworkers, and relatives looking at him in a new light, heaping him with praise and adulation for making a wonderful decision and for "joining the club." (After all, no married guy wants his friends to be single for too long, lest it pull their friendships apart any further, which is why we suggested that in order to close the deal you and your man hang out with your married friends. See, it works!)

Suddenly he may be seen confidently snapping his suspenders (although if he wears suspenders, you may want to reconsider accepting), kicking back with a new air of manliness, and appraising the value of the engagement gifts like a seasoned eBayer. This confidence and euphoria should last until together you arrive at the next phase, Committing to Concrete Wedding Plans.

Of course, he may have an altogether different experience. While visions of color schemes and china patterns may be floating through your mind, he may be second-guessing his decision and using the engagement period to reflect on the relationship, now that there's a promise of a real commitment. This is only one more reason that you need to continue to practice all of the positive, beneficial habits you've learned from us and keep breaking those questionable practices. Let's take a look at a couple that recently went through this and find out if they came out the other side Mr. and Mrs. or Mr. and Ms.

Harold and Jennifer

AFTER AN EIGHT-YEAR COURTSHIP, Harold and Jennifer became engaged, despite the objections of his two older sisters, who thought Jennifer was too bossy and materialistic. Jennifer had never felt accepted by Harold's sisters and would often vent and make divisive remarks about them behind their backs to Harold or his friends. Once Harold popped the question, though, Jennifer's confidence grew. Jennifer felt that she was "golden" now that she had finally received a family ring, especially after "paying her dues" for almost a decade. Her new confidence, coupled with her hurt feelings, led her to act out against her future sisters-in-law (as opposed to simply ranting in private to Harold), and as the wedding neared, Jennifer's desire to spite the sisters grew and her actions became more and more vocal. At a family function, after one too many glasses of wine, when one of the sisters voiced an objection to Jennifer's statements about Harold's financial situation, Jennifer said quite loudly, "He may be your brother, but he's my fiancé, so butt out."

At a private family meeting shortly thereafter, Harold's sisters, mother, and grandmother all banded together to protect "their Harold" from Jennifer's "bad influence." Harold couldn't disagree with their "sudden" assessment of her inflammatory and materialistic character. As Jennifer started acting out their private battles in public, he saw his family unit crumbling right before his eyes. Harold broke the engagement because he felt that Jennifer had started abusing her privileges (and his sisters) once they'd become engaged, and he didn't like what he saw. Some time after cutting Jennifer loose, Harold became engaged to one of his sister's best friends!

As our friend Karin said in her interview, your man is yours, but he's not all yours, even if he's professed his undying love to you. Don't forget it.

But What About All These Strange Feelings *I'm* Having?

AND WHAT ABOUT YOU? THIS IS THE MOMENT you've been dreaming of, right? Well, it's not that simple. Closing the deal never is. While some women actually enjoy the engagement process and find it exhilarating, others buckle under the pressure. Whether it's the dissatisfaction with the engagement ring setting (get over it!) or the stress of whom you're going to leave out of your bridal party, anything can become an issue, and what might seem trivial to some men may be a huge issue for some women.

It doesn't help that when most men are getting slapped on the back, you may be getting pressure to set the date and deal with the plans (yes, it's still usually the gals who do the planning). You may have relatives (i.e., your mother or his) who have their own ideas about everything *they've* been dreaming about for you, for the last X number of years, or you may be dealing with friends or relatives who are happy for you yet sad for themselves. A friend we know *actually* told her relatives at their engagement party, "This is a happy day for you but a sad day for me." Talk about hailing on a parade! Changes in family/marital status can sometimes make single relatives or friends evaluate their own status, and if this reaction occurs, our best advice is to try to be the bigger person and understand how they feel. (And, of course, get them a copy of this book!) After all, you are the happy one.

Engagement Explosions

PLANNING AN ENGAGEMENT PARTY OR DINner, meeting the relatives, and integrating two families can be difficult even under the best of circumstances. You may find yourself with a virtual powder keg of **Engagement Explosives.** Very often couples that have never fought can start bickering over some relatively small issues that suddenly seem insurmountable. Many men and women start to see their intended through a fresh lens by the way they handle (or don't handle) the stress. Your fiancé, given his newly acquired sense of self-esteem and calm, may even view your stress as being volatile and emotional. Even with the lessons you have learned about controlling your 'tude, it sounds like the honeymoon could be over before it's even begun, right?

What to do? It can be a stressful time, especially because you and he both probably also want to put on a good show for everyone. Realize that what you're going through may be new to you but many couples have been there before you, so there *are* solutions. Our advice: Try to approach all the new stress with a sense of humor. Why not set a dinner date where both of you have to prepare and deliver the worst wedding toast of all time? The important point here is to keep it light.

Don't be afraid of confronting the really hard stuff before you walk down the aisle. While there's comfort in knowing you're engaged, there's also the relief that you're *not* married yet. There are so many issues to deal with during the engagement process that both of you should remember that there's an escape hatch. Believe it or not, keeping this in mind often creates a better environment and less pressure when it comes to sorting out issues.

So, considering your current state of mind, let's take a look at the greatest potential land mines and how one should disarm them.

La Famiglia

You've realized (with our help) that you don't marry only your fiancé; in many cases, you marry his entire family too. We dealt with a different aspect of this in our multiculti chapter, but now that you are officially engaged, your family's involvement will have much more impact because the marriage is on its way.

Let us reiterate that your loyalty and your fiancé's loyalty are to *each other*. That's a non-negotiable clause of any healthy relationship. Unfortunately, this won't help to resolve the problems that will arise when his sister-in-law refuses your invitation to be in your wedding party, or when his mom is too opinionated or his dad makes you sit on his lap during Thanksgiving dinner. You must remember the following things before attempting to resolve any of this:

○ Your family isn't a walk in the park either.
○ They're his family and they're not going anywhere.

- Odds are the feelings are mutual.
- He will love you so much more if you can make it work. (Remember this throughout the process. It has saved more relationships than you can imagine.)

Even simple, joyful things, like deciding on a china pattern, can cause drama. All involved need to be on their best behavior before the deal is closed. Don't assume that his family has finished evaluating you (they'll be doing that the rest of your life, honey!). Be patient and understanding. Don't let any issues stay unresolved. Whether he didn't ask your father for your hand or his mother wants to share the grand family history with you (childhood keepsakes, sports photos, recipes), find the time to work it out before you walk down the aisle. We always find that when it comes to family, the easiest thing to do is the right thing. Being the bigger person isn't always easy, but it pays dividends in the long run. As previously discussed, there's nothing wrong with giving family members a little "client service," especially when you want to make it to the honeymoon. And don't forget to keep smiling— you've just snagged the man of your dreams!

Cash: The Wedding and Other Money Woes

Who's got what and how they handle it can also blow a deal right up to the "I do's," whether you're marrying poor and he's marrying rich or it's the other way around; whether his father holds money over your fiancé's head and your family thinks talking about money is distasteful; whether you want his family to split the wedding with your parents and his parents are old fashioned and think the girl's parents should pay for the whole thing— money trouble can lead to big deal-closing trouble.

While you were in the dating phase, the expenses you shared might have been minimal and your behavior must have demonstrated enough responsibility that he felt comfortable enough with you to move forward. If you were a big shopper and could afford to be, or your fiancé loved to shop too and didn't worry, he might never have said one word about your spending habits. But if your spending was a concern for him in any way and he commented on it at any point preengagement, then don't think that this issue won't arise now. You should be thinking in terms of *both* of your finances and your future.

Whether it's planning an engagement party or wedding or talking about housing, suddenly the money monster can rear its ugly head. With the cost of weddings rising each year, the "dream" wedding can often take on unrealistic proportions. How far you or your fiancé push for the "perfect wedding" may result in a debt-laden, stress-laden honeymoon, and that's never a good start to a marriage. Our advice (and that of the people we spoke to): Create and stick to a budget and don't let anyone force you into the uncomfortable zone.

Even if you were completely in sync with how to spend while dating, money will probably become an issue involving your families in planning the big day. We suggest that each of you deal directly with your own set of parents. If he needs to request some monetary help from his family, let him do it and don't say a word to them. Our logic behind this is that until you and he say "I do," you're not family yet and your request for funds may come off as inappropriate and demanding. (Especially for those parental units who believe the "early days" *should* be "the hungry years" and a bit of a struggle.) A request by either party for more money for a "caviar bar" will be read as fiscally irresponsible.

Whether he's exceptionally successful or on unemployment insurance or whether you are a successful CEO or haven't worked since . . . ever, most money issues can be resolved if you can maintain proper respect for each other and don't make money the focus of your relationship. Of course, don't skirt this sensitive subject and the very personal feelings you may have about money—you must keep the channels of communication open. One last thing: If one of you is in debt, please find a way to handle this issue before you become legal, as this can get out of control once you are married, when your credit histories will be forever joined and you can ruin each other's credit rating.

What We Hope You Take with You   Have a direct discussion about money, even if the issue hasn't come up yet. Start out by saying that it's an uncomfortable subject to talk about but that you need to. Tell him that you want to try to find a solution before you get your families involved. If you know right away that you'll need to bring in your parents, then map out a plan of attack. (Only you know your families.) Above all, be cool, communicative, and compromising.

The Prenup

Congratulations—your fiancé's loaded or maybe you are, and one of you wants a prenup. Obviously, you've navigated this battle successfully through the dating phase, but now that you're talking about commingling assets, the discrepancy in the bank accounts will be all the more apparent.

Prenups come in many shapes and forms. There are some strong legal arguments for them and some strong emotional arguments against them. We don't need to discuss whether or not prenuptial agreements are right or wrong. The only time a prenup is an issue is when one party wants one and one doesn't.

So let's say your fiancé is loaded and wants to discuss an arrangement and you don't like the idea. After all, you (like every other person who doesn't want to sign a prenup) will say, "If marriage is forever, then why would you go forward if there were any doubts?" Or the ever popular "I feel like I'm negotiating my *divorce* before I'm even married." You wonder if he is going to move forward without one in place or if you can persuade yourself to go forward with one in place. Or if he really loves you.

Our advice: If one party wants a prenup, then get all the counseling help you want to deal with this issue. After all, if neither party feels that the prenup issue was resolved to mutual satisfaction, the seeds will be planted to haunt the relationship and will surface, even in years to come. We've seen it happen. The quicker you can navigate through this uncomfortable process, the better it will be for both of you and the relationship. Once again, the golden rule is to make sure that both parties are happy or comfortable with the final document. If either side feels slighted, you're in for trouble. Work it out now or you have a greater chance of needing to work out your divorce settlement later.

Of course, *what* you do is up to you. *How* you do it is up to us. We can assure you that it must be done with dignity and restraint. Remember what we said about the ring being a means and *not* an end? Well, that applies, all the time, not just for some of it. And it applies to his money and yours. So express your concerns, stick to the facts, and stay rational. Since both of you obviously want to close the deal, you will both have incentive to work out this little part of the big deal. Keep in mind that the prenup negotiations might last only a little while but any bad vibes will linger forever. Three things to remember: (1) A good prenup can protect you; (2) a badly arranged prenup can sow the seeds for a bad relationship; and (3) An ill-timed prenup is as bad as a bad prenup, so discuss and settle it all early.

We know many couples who got prenups and are thrilled and in love, and others who wished they'd handled things differently. We both believe in prenups only when there are real wealth issues or children involved. Here's one example of a couple who didn't know our three prenup pointers.

Blaine and Thomas

BLAINE AND THOMAS RECENTLY WENT THROUGH a painful divorce. A pretty, stylish, and elegant brunette who lives on the West Coast, Blaine can trace her troubled marriage to the one-sided prenup and her husband's emotional and financial stinginess. Blaine met Thomas when she was in her late twenties, and after a yearlong relationship they became engaged. Her family planned a magnificent wedding, which was put in jeopardy when Thomas thrust a one-sided prenup at her right before the wedding day. Blaine and her family were shocked and upset. Although his previous marriage had ended in divorce and Thomas may have been justifiably nervous, his unexpected ultimatum threw a damper on the impending nuptials.

The discussions grew angry, with accusations and recriminations, causing Blaine to call off the wedding and return all the gifts. A few months later Thomas tried to win her back, and despite her parents' protestations Blaine agreed, mainly because she was in love, thought he was suitable, and wanted to close the deal.

Ten years and two children later, Thomas informed Blaine he wanted a divorce on their wedding anniversary and proceeded to try to shaft her in her divorce settlement, uprooting her and the children from their house to an apartment. Blaine, older and wiser, admits to this day that her focus was on closing the deal. While they did have some nice moments together—and two children—she realized that she should have opened her eyes and seen what she now sees—that Thomas never changed.

What We Hope You Take with You While Blaine and Thomas are an extreme case, the manner in which Thomas and his family handled getting the prenup was a testament to his general attitude (and possibly his feelings). Blaine's overlooking negative behavior because she was in love or because she just wanted to close the deal was an error in judgment in the past. If Thomas truly loved her, he'd have been willing to try to work it all out. Look at what's in front of you and be honest with yourself. Don't sweep negative behavior under the carpet—as you may end up in a filthy divorce.

THOUGH WE HAVE TRIED to advise you on the rules of engagement, we also don't want to rain on your very sunny parade. Remember, our goal here isn't to tell you everything will be fine but to try to let you look at the situation and deal with it to ensure that things *will* have a better chance of turning out that way.

Endnote

We Hope the Coaching Helped

LIKE ANY TOP ATHLETE OR BUSINESS PERson, sometimes you need a coach who can set you back on track toward your goals. We hope that on your quest for everlasting love and commitment you found our advice helpful and considered it with honest self-evaluation (and a smile or two). If from this book you only take a few things with you into your relationship, we hope confidence, a positive attitude, some self-restraint, a sense of humor, and the determined pursuit of a deep and gratifying love affair are among them.

When we began to write a book that we hoped would help women navigate the treacherous dating waters that sink relationships before they enter the safe marriage harbor, we agreed that we wanted to convey, first and foremost, that the endgame must be a healthy, meaningful, and deeply committed relationship, not marriage in and of itself. Don't get us wrong: While marriage is nothing more than a public acknowledgment of a very private affair, it is still the foundation for many wonderful and important things.

There may be unique issues that you and your partner will face that we haven't specifically covered in these pages. Not to worry. All too often, it is not the solutions themselves but the time spent finding them that strengthen and move relationships forward.

After reading this book, you should have the skills required to seek whatever answers you are looking for.

So here's to your success on your journey to the altar and afterward. It takes a brave woman to stop and ask for directions. You're on your way.

Glossary

Bediquette (n.): The proper rules of behavior when you have a sleepover with your man.

The Bluff (n.): The act of breaking up with your boyfriend who won't commit, yet keeping the door open should he change his mind (see Chapter 8).

Coitus Argumentus (n.): Arguments that occur during sex, usually about what one partner wants or prefers.

Commitia (n.): A type of VD (vow disavowal) causing men to be incapable of commitment.

Cutting Bait (v.): The act of breaking up and shutting the door for good.

Dating Inflection Point (D.I.P.) (n.): A moment in time when you evaluate the status of your relationship.

Engagement Euphoria (n.): The mind-set of a postproposal man involving a tremendous sense of relief, usually displayed through an overwhelming expression of excitement.

Engagement Explosives (n., pl.): Fireworks from all the pent-up emotion that occur when you finally get engaged.

Engagement Purgatory (n.): The moment preceding a man's proposal in which he weighs his decision.

FASSS (n.): Fat ASS Syndrome. A condition in which a woman believes (usually wrongly, might we add) that her ass is too large for her man.

Fellationship (n.): A relationship based on little but the act of fellatio. (Courtesy of Robinne Lee.)

Gold and Diamond Life Preserver (n.): Engagement ring.

Level (n.): Your position or rank in terms of compatibility as a couple.

Man with a Plan (n.): A guy who's ready, willing, able, and prepared to get married.

Marriage Maneuver (v.): To put out feelers to establish what strategy you'll have to utilize to get him to propose.

Marriage Maneuvering (n.): Behavior intended to determine where your man stands on the marriage front.

Marriage Momentum (n.): A force that gradually builds as the couple gets closer to marriage and the boyfriend becomes a Man with a Plan.

Marriage Motivator: The buttons to push in order to achieve Marriage Momentum, thus propelling him to the altar.

Monopolygamist (n.): One who goes on too many first dates.

Overdating (v.): Setting your sights too high with a guy who will never commit to you. *Related term:* Overdater (n.): One who overdates.

Playa Hata (n.): An individual who dwells on the negative. *Plural: Playa Hataz. Related term: Playa hatin'* (v.)

P.N.P. (n.): Positive-Negative-Positive. An effective method used to deliver bad news by couching it between good news. (Courtesy of Phyllis George.)

Polymonogamist (n.): One with a history of long-term relationships.

Rock on a Ring (n.): Engagement ring.

Scheherazade Factor (n.): The creation of mystery at critical junctures in a relationship with the objective of leaving your date wanting more (see Chapter 6).

Speech Spin (n.): Recycling or repackaging the way you relay information; remarketing your past, present, and future in a more positive light.

Tefloning (v.): Avoiding a topic (usually marriage) in conversation.

Ultimatum (n.): Something that a girl should rarely if ever give to force or bully a guy into proposing.

Underdating (v.): Dating someone below your level; one who does not challenge you. *Related term:* Underdater (n.): One who underdates.

Womanity (n.): The female subspecies of humankind, a.k.a. "the ladies."

Yapper Syndrome (n.): A complex in which a woman leaves aspects of her life open and visible to all, leaving nothing to the imagination; opposite of Scheherazade. *Synonym:* Yapperitis (inflammation of the yapper).

Acknowledgments

WE COULDN'T HAVE CLOSED THE DEAL ON *Closing the Deal* without the help and support of many people.

Thank you to our deal closers of another kind, uber-agents Suzanne Gluck and Jonathan Pecarsky at William Morris. You rule.

Thanks to the best kick-ass editor that two guys could ask for: Joelle Yudin. You went above the call of duty and we adore you, your vitality, and smarts.

A big thanks to the marketing and publicity mavens Karen Resnick, Pamela Spengler-Jaffe, Debbie Stier, and Diana Tynan at HarperCollins and Liz Anklow and Juliet Horn at Dan Klores Communications—we know you're so good because you make it look so easy.

We want to especially thank the women we interviewed for this book. We are indebted to you! Thank you, Phyllis George, Adriana Trigiani, Patty Stegman, Carla Rubin, Shirley Travis, Karin Wilzig, Ruth Campanelli, Mary Blose, Lorre Erlick, Gina Keir, Andrea Glimcher, Atoosa Rubenstein, and Judy Licht.

We also want to thank our superstar cartoonist Marisa Acocella Marchetto. You are not only a fabulous woman but also officially an extraordinary deal closer. Congrats!

—R.K. and D.R.

From Daniel: Thank you to the many people who have positively influenced my life over the years, especially if you made me laugh.

I give my deepest gratitude to my magnificent, beautiful, and intelligent wife Leora. You generously gave up nearly every Saturday night for a year without complaint and were unflinchingly supportive of me throughout the writing of this book. You are the magic and music of my life and I feel so fortunate to have found you and made you mine. I love you without end.

To my daughter, Natasha, thank you for filling my life with sunshine and reminding me to take nothing for granted. I love you, little bear.

To Mom and Dad: If I do half the things for Natasha that you have done for me, she will be a very lucky young lady. I love you both the same.

Thank you to my sister (and a half!) Louise: You are as selfless as they come and have taught me many lessons in life and I love you for that. I couldn't ask for a better sibling. Thank you to the Bloch family, especially my mother-in-law, Barbara, for making me feel as though I deserve your daughter and to Garth for your big heart. To the Bloch, Daniels, Goddard, Rudman, Samson, Selbo, Smidt, and Rosenberg families—thank you for being such a giving and supportive extended family.

Thanks to my writing partner and close friend, Richard, even though as of this writing you haven't included me in your "final" acknowledgments. I hope you will continue to serve as my therapist, corporate coach, financial adviser, and friend for many years to come. It's no secret that your alter ego is Supermensch.

Thank you to my colleagues at Revolution Studios who make making movies as much fun and rewarding as it should be. Specifically, my deep gratitude to our fearless leader, supreme deal closer, and my friend, Elaine Goldsmith-Thomas, whose passion for work and drive to succeed has been a powerful inspiration for over a decade.

And a special thank you to Brad Aston, Robbie Brenner, Alti and Sarla Bukiet, Sonya and Steven Cantor, Cristina and Chris Cuomo, Tanya and Clinton Ephron, Rowan Farber, Patti Felker, Maura and Russ Gewirtz, Amy and David Hochman, Rachael Horovitz, Kerry Kane, Robinne Lee, Hilary Swank and Chad Lowe, Marla Maples, Shary Moalemzadeh, Carol O'Connell, Guy Penini, Andy and Taly Russell, Deb Schindler, Shira-Lee Shalit, Ricky Strauss, Eric Suddelson, Susan and Barry Tatelman, Dan Thomas, Dana and Jeffrey Unger, Marcy, Michael, and Andrew Warren, Jonathan Weisgal, and to my American, Canadian, English, and South African family and friends.

From Richard: I want to thank all those people who make my life so rich and fulfilling.

I also dedicate this book to my late mother, Marilyn, and my late grandmothers, Elsie and Anna, who with all of my female relatives "trained" me to be a good husband and father.

I'm also dedicating this book to the CEO of my life, my wife, Dana, the most gorgeous, intelligent, and wonderful woman I have ever met. I am a better person since knowing you. Thank you for closing the deal with me. To the world's best children, Talia, Lucas, and Georgia: You are an inspiration to me. I love you "this much."

Dad and Phyllis, you are both the world's greatest and a true inspiration as a couple. I love you both very much. Susan, I love and respect all you have done and continue to do. I can always count on you for a good laugh and a dose of reality. Marcia, you are not my mother-in-law, you are my second mother!

A special note of thanks to my business partner at kirshenbaum bond & partners, Jonathan, and his lovely wife, Rebecca Bradshaw Bond. You are both so special to me.

Thank you to Muffie and Sherrell Aston, Carla Rubin and Georgios Avramopoulos, Keith and Melina Bellows, Carole

Brodie-Gelles, Ruth and Rocco Campanelli, Rosemarie Ryan and Ben Dyatt, Lorinda Ash and Peter Ezersky, Fred and Cookie Geier, Phyllis George, Marc and Andrea Glimcher, Stephen and Stephanie Gottlieb, Gina and Andy Kier, Dr. Joseph Klinkov, Marisa and Silvano Marchetto, Rabbi Adam and Sharon Mintz, Lisa Mirchin, David and Jamie Mitchell, Miles Nadal, Jordan and Stephanie Schur, Bippy and Jackie Siegal, Stephanie Greenfield and Mitchell Silverman, Patty and Danny Stegman, Adriana Trigani and Tim Stephenson, Rebecca and Chuck Asher Walsh, Karin and Alan Wilzig—and to the world's best executive assistant Carol O'Connell: I couldn't have done it without you! I am deeply grateful.

And lastly to my dear friend, great writing partner, and one of the quickest and creative minds around, Daniel Rosenberg. I know you think I forgot to thank you in my acknowledgments (okay, I saw yours and you guilted me into it so here it is). My definition of partner is "the other side of the coin; someone who makes you better, someone who makes you laugh, $1 + 1 = 3$." I guess that makes us great partners.